Karen F. Marheim

MRS. PREACHER

MRS. PREACHER

Succeeding As a Minister's Wife

For Those in the Parsonage and the Pew

Karen Norheim

College Press Publishing Company, Joplin, Missouri

Copyright © 1985
College Press Publishing Company
Second Printing, May 1988

Printed and bound in the
United States of America

Cover Illustration By Paula Nash

Scripture references are from the King James Version and The New English Bible as noted.

Library of Congress Catalog Card Number: 84-073302
International Standard Book Number: 0-89900-204-8

ACKNOWLEDGMENTS

Anyone who has ever written a book knows it can't be done without a lot of cooperation from many people, and this book is no exception. Approximately 250 ministers' wives across the country have openly shared their hopes, dreams, and frustrations either in person or through a detailed Preacher's Wife Questionnaire. Nearly 250 church members from coast to coast have also willingly participated in a Church Survey regarding the minister's wife and her role in the church. To them all I am deeply grateful for their honesty: it is truly their book.

I am also indebted to Professor Larry Keen, Dr. Bruce Parmenter, Dr. Dallas E. Shafer, Dr. Paul Benjamin, Dr. Paul Boatman, and to Dr. LeRoy Lawson and Dr. James Girdwood for their counsel and assistance.

Lastly, I am indebted to my family: my daughters, Jennifer, Angela and Terri who did extra housework, cooking, stamping, folding and addressing envelopes for the survey; to my husband Neil, who from the beginning encouraged me to do this research and writing, giving helpful suggestions and insights along the way; to my parents, Andrew and Nellie Larson, for the privilege of being reared in a Christian home and teaching me to love the church and her leaders.

PREFACE

I am an incurable fan of ministers' wives. Having been married to one for a quarter of a century, I have no doubt that God selected only his finest stuff to make these special creations. Even as a young man I realized that my job was not as demanding as my wife's. That's why I've worked pretty hard to keep her around. I would hate to be trying to survive without her!

Many men who aren't in the ministry can write such a tribute of their wives, of course. I don't mean to suggest that we should all pity the poor parson's wife, because "nobody knows the trouble she's seen." That would be carrying the case too far. There are, after all, several compensations in her role, not the least of which is that she gets to be married to a minister!

But that's the rub, isn't it? Not all ministers are equal, and not a one of them is perfect. It isn't my most pleasant memory to recall Joy's and my early years together, as I watched her growing disenchantment—with her man and with her role. She wanted—and needed—to be more than Mrs. Preacher. She struggled to find acceptable ways for her God-implanted gifts to be used in His service while at the same time assisting her less-than-perfect spouse fulfill his ministry while at the same time never losing consciousness of the staring eyes of the church upon her while at the same time. . . .

That she came through those difficult years and has kept on maturing into my ideal of a minister's wife is a tribute to her strength and God's unfailing love. It is also because we have been blessed through the years with supportive, considerate, and generous congregations.

We have never experienced some of the horrors Karen Norheim discusses so helpfully here. We have served among some of God's finest people, and they have saved us much heartache. But we have friends in the ministry who could have supplied Karen with additional evidence that all is not paradise in the parsonage. Here is a book that needs to be read by all church leaders charged with the care and feeding of the parsonage family. Ministers and their wives should not demand preferential treatment; however, they have every reason to expect Christian concern from their congregations. Mrs. Norheim helps churches know how to express that concern.

I like Karen. She and Neil have loved their service to the Lord and have never stopped loving each other while serving. They have kept their sense of humor and that indispensable perspective that true servants of Christ must have, in order to distinguish the Lord's commission from the people's innumerable commands.

The Norheims remind me of something every minister, faced with the confusing diversity of demands upon him, must learn or despair: when one becomes a "professional" minister, it does not matter so much which of the many specialties he develops, nor what specific kind of formal education he has completed, nor even what charismatic abilities he possesses. The making of a minister consists of the making of the man. He offers himself to God and His people. He rises or falls on his Christlike character more than on anything else.

You can be a sterling lawyer and a bad man; you can be a famous surgeon and a bad man; you can be a television or movie star with a fabulous income and still be a bad man. But a bad man can never be a true minister of the Gospel.

Nor can the minister's wife get away with being a bad woman. There is no formula for success in the parsonage except the one for success in the pulpit. Preparing for the ministry, for husband or wife, means preparing to be a whole person before God, on behalf of God, among God's people. It consists of being more than doing, of believing more than bedazzling, and of loving more than being loved. Yes, it means being criticized, misunderstood, and unappreciated. But it also means seeing, feeling, and growing through every endeavor somehow to personify and publish glad tidings.

Thanks, Karen, for giving both Mrs. Preacher and her dependent husband this helpful study.

E. LeRoy Lawson
Central Christian Church
Mesa, Arizona

CONTENTS

INTRODUCTION

Have you ever wondered what is in a name? Or have you ever played the word association game in which a word is given, and you must respond with the first word that comes to mind? Let's play that game right now! Take for instance, the words, "Preacher's Wife." What is your immediate knee-jerk reaction? Be honest now. Is it a positive or a negative reaction? Ask yourself, "Why did I immediately respond in a positive (or negative) way?" This may at first seem a frivolous exercise to you, but first reactions can be an indication of deeper feelings you may have on a given subject.

Consider the following examples of reactions I've experienced as a minister's wife:

When I was a senior in high school I made the decision to attend a Bible seminary. Shortly after a request to have my transcript sent to this college, the principal called me into his office to discuss the matter. He urged me to go to a "better" college, for he felt I would only be wasting my intelligence and time there, and might end up marrying only a minister! He attended a church, so church life was not foreign to him, but nevertheless he felt he should "save" me from an unwise decision. This was my first negative reaction experienced toward ministers' wives.

Another incident happened as I was working in a factory office while my husband was finishing his education. A man expressed his opinion that I didn't measure up to his concept of what ministers' wives should be. Upon questioning him, he revealed his concept to be that of a dowdy, draggy, drably and indistinctly dressed woman, very often pregnant, worn out, and followed by a whole passel of kids. This I also added to my list of reactions toward the minister's wife.

Not too long ago I attended an older Sunday School class in order to get better acquainted with the members. When I sat down beside a lady she immediately froze and looked straight ahead until the class period ended. Afterward she apologized for not speaking to me, because she felt so flustered and nervous with me beside her. What is that illusive quality preachers' wives have which make people react in this way? Another item for my list.

My best illustration to date comes from a recent visit to a specialist recommended by our family doctor. When he entered the examination room, he had nothing to say; he just began examining all my various and assorted parts. As he was making all those appropriate aahhs and hmmmms that doctors do, he said, "I see you're a minister's wife!" I couldn't resist responding with, "Oh, don't tell me it's showing there too!" He was rather nonplussed at that.

Add these illustrations to notions that the minister's wife should know how to sing and play the piano, to speak at a moment's notice, to be a leader among the women, to practically be all things to all women, a kind of "super woman." Add also the good notions from people who love the minister's wife and encourage her to be herself. They realize the diversity of people who look upon the minister's wife as "Pastor's Wife," "the Reverend's Mrs.," or the "Preacher's Wife" as opposed to seeing her as an individual in her own right.

In one church where we ministered they affectionately referred to me as "Reverend Mom." My husband was "Reverend Dad" and my daughters were "Rev. Daughter #1, Rev. Daughter #2, and Rev. Daughter #3. Last summer a young seminary student, serving as an intern with our church, frequently ate meals with us. Upon hearing that we were referred to in this way he said, "Well, do you think I'll be called Rev. Son One soon?!" He was catching the idea that we can gracefully wear titles others give to us (and even humorously at times) without it becoming a point of contention or of feeling we are forced into certain role expectations. Ministers' wives have the option of letting the "Preacher's Wife Pedestal" become a stepping stone or a stumbling block in their ministry.

Now go back and re-evaluate your feelings toward ministers' wives. Your reaction will probably indicate your deeper feelings about them, based on your past experiences with certain ones, or attitudes of others which have influenced you. The reason why delving into your feelings in this matter is important, is that they reflect your concept of the church as a body. It stands to reason that the body (the church) cannot be whole or function efficiently and properly if certain members do not work together with other members, regardless of their roles in church life.

For instance, consider the physical body. What happens if the feet become jealous of the mouth because it is eloquent? Or the internal organs refuse to work because only the actions of the visible members are noticed? Or the lungs quit working because it's just assumed they will? It is almost ridiculous to ask. Of course the whole body suffers when one of its parts is gone or is not functioning properly. Spiritually, the whole body working together to accomplish God's plan is certainly more superior to some body parts having to work overtime to compensate for others, thus becoming exhausted prematurely, or other parts which rebel and spread poison throughout the body. Thus, when one part suffers, all parts suffer.

It is beginning to appear that the body part called "Preacher's Wife" is suffering. Some visibly, some internally.

This book has as its aim to provoke church members and ministers' wives alike to examine their inner feelings and outer responses regarding the role of the minister's wife and her relationship to the church and her husband's ministry.

The following chapters contain results from a national survey taken among ministers' wives. You'll find out where they hurt the most and what they enjoy the most. You'll also read the results from a national church survey which reveals just exactly what church members expect of and are looking for in a minister's wife. There are some interviews with Christian counselors who offer some common factors, peculiar to the ministry, which lead to problems and sometimes a breakdown in the marriages. It also includes ways in which churches can encourage and minister to their minister's wife, and ways in which ministers' wives can minister to the churches.

REFLECTIONS

1. Give a definition for the role of minister's wife.
2. Is this definition what your church expects of the minister's wife?
3. Do you consider the minister's wife to be a "permanent" part of the church body, or just a temporary one? Why?
4. Would you like to be a close friend of the minister's wife? Why or why not?
5. Would you encourage your son or daughter to be a minister or minister's wife? Why or why not?
6. Would you describe your church as a preacher's wife lover or a preacher's wife hater? What might be the root cause for a love/hate relationship, and some possible solutions?
7. Do you think the unity and effectiveness of your church can hinge upon its concept of or relationship to the minister's wife? In what ways?
8. What ingredients are needed to achieve a good "marriage" between the minister's family and the church?

1

BEFORE YOU SAY "I DO"

Everyone will agree it is much better to train long before you step into the ring. Fortunate indeed is the young woman who seeks to prepare herself in every way possible BEFORE saying "I do" to the next Billy Graham. Of course, there are some things that cannot be learned until you're actually there, but many things you can. It is a little like marriage: you prepare all you can, expecting great things, but some things you will never learn until you've actually been there.

If you are attending a Bible seminary and intend to marry a minister (if God so wills), here are some questions to ask yourself:

1. Why do I want to marry a minister?
2. Can I handle criticism—am I willing to live in a "fish bowl"?
3. Am I willing to move whenever and wherever my husband thinks we should?
4. Can I share him with everyone else, sometimes having my needs wait until others are helped?

5. Am I strong enough to be a "one-parent family" in regard to raising the children mostly by myself?
6. Do I have a servant attitude? Am I also "called" to ministry as he is?
7. Am I more ambitious than he is? Would I always have to "push" him?
8. Am I relatively new in the faith? Is he? Are we both mature enough for such heavy responsibility now?
9. Can I live simply, i.e., "on a shoestring" if need be?
10. Do I have to give up an education for marriage? If so, will I resent it later?
11. Am I committed to the man—not the title?

This list certainly isn't exhaustive, but it will start your thinking. After you have honestly examined yourself, your desires and motives, seek out an older minister's wife whom you respect and get first hand information of what it's like to be a minister's wife. Ask her about the joys as well as the heartaches. If you come to the conclusion it's not for you, for your sake, and that of the church, let your preacher-husband-to-be know before you tie the knot. Don't try to change him or think he'll change his mind about ministry once he's married to you. If you start out this way your marriage will be in jeopardy before it has hardly begun. He may grow to despise you for making him choose between you and the ministry, or despise himself for his own weakness.

Many are the men who went to seminary and for a smile and pretty face sold their dreams of ministry down the river. This is not to say pretty faces don't make it in the ministry, but they should not be the most important criteria a ministerial student seeks in a wife.

Paul Benjamin, in *The Vision Splendid* says, "Occasionally a minister marries a spoiled and selfish prima donna who will brook no rivals. His work is a constant threat to her. She will do everything possible to get her husband to leave the ministry if his work interferes with her whims. Then she is just as unhappy with his next profession. . . . a minister may find out to his great sorrow someday that he has been deceived by charm and beauty (Prov. 31:30). He may pay a tremendous emotional price for a pretty face."[1]

---

1. Paul Benjamin, *The Vision Splendid* (Washington, D.C.: National Church Growth Research Center, The American Press, 1981), p. 19.

To any young seminarians reading this, I challenge you to look for a wife who is mature both spiritually and emotionally. Find one who is capable of an intimate and warm personal relationship, who is emotionally stable, who has an independent personality (you won't always be around to help), and who shares the same view of ministry you do. The importance of chastity to your marriage, your ministry, your self-esteem, and future attitude of sex within marriage should not be underestimated. Plan together when you will start a family—before or after education is completed. You may stretch yourself too thin trying to support a wife and family as well as paying for an education. Married students miss some of the college life. If your wife must give up her education to support you as you finish schooling, the price may prove too high. She may feel cheated and resentful. Not a very promising prospect for beginning marriage or a ministry, is it? Your wife must be a believer (II Cor. 6:14-17) and preferably not a new Christian. Although not necessary, I view some college education as a definite help. Not necessarily because churches expect it of her, but for her own self-esteem. Mary Bouma, a minister's wife who has authored several articles and a book about minister's wives, views college as a necessity for the minister's wife. In her research she found a definite link between college education and feelings of self-worth among minister's wives.

College courses for the minister's wife can prepare her for teaching and leading, and broaden her view. College life teaches her social skills in getting along with people of various backgrounds and temperaments. But most of all it gives her a feeling of accomplishment, and a sense of self-worth and preparedness.

It would be foolish to say young women lacking these qualities will never be successful in the ministry, for that would indeed be limiting the possibilities of the Holy Spirit working in their lives. However, one should engage the head as well as the heart in such an important decision as marriage. Your decision will have long-lasting effects both for you and the churches you serve. One day the heart might falter in the stress of living and the head may have to assert itself until such time that the threat may pass. So choose well. Better to make haste slowly rather than to repent at leisure when it comes to choosing a wife.

19

Therefore, minister-to-be or minister's-wife-to-be, carefully weigh all the circumstances and questions before you say "I do." Seek help and guidance from older ones in the ministry. Honestly examine yourselves, your motives and ideals. Take advantage of college courses or seminars designed to help prepare you for ministry. This is not just a career you are choosing—it's a different way of life with extra responsibilities and qualifications because of the position you will hold. Pray earnestly over it and seek God's guidance with both head and heart, for there will be eternal consequences both for you and the church. Much hangs in the balance.

For those readers who think young prospective ministers' wives should only be told of the joys and blessings of ministry for fear of disillusioning them, let me pose these questions. If you had a daughter preparing for marriage and she asked you how it really was, what would you tell her? Would you tell her it was all joy and roses, or would you try to prepare her for the hardships and pitfalls as well? If you only told her how wonderful it was, would she resent it after she discovered life is not one big fairytale? Would she become disillusioned with marriage because hers wasn't what you said it would be? Would she think you dishonest for not preparing her adequately when you knew the truth? And if you had given her a balanced account of marriage—good and bad—would it have deterred her from marriage? Probably not. Marriage is here to stay, just as many women will opt for being a minister's wife regardless of the pitfalls.

Research among ministers' wives revealed that many young wives are leveling charges against the older ministers' wives. They're saying the older ones are afraid to admit they're human too, or that the life of the minister's wife is not all roses and glory as they've been led to believe. They're accusing us of hypocrisy among our ranks, that we're not telling it like it is. Perhaps with these accusations against the older women, they are just being as a woman who has forgotten the pain of childbirth—they don't intentionally leave it out, it's just not too important when you see the finished product.

We all know there are eternal consequences hanging in the balance over the relationship between the church and the minister's wife. It is serious business, and no place for the frivolous or dewy-eyed maiden, to be embraced upon a romantic whim. It does get pretty windy up there on that pedestal. Rocks do sometimes get thrown at that glass house we live in. We need to be transparent enough to admit it, and to share how we're coping with it. The majority of the ministers' wives who participated in the survey were open and transparent about the joys and blessings of ministry as well as the sorrows and heartaches. That's what this book is all about. Let it encourage, equip and challenge you to mature as a minister's wife, to truly "grace" the parsonage. Let it also open some honest communication between the minister's wife and the church that together they might enhance each other's ministry and the building up of the church.

REFLECTIONS

1. What are some positive reasons a young woman might consider for marrying a minister?
2. What are some negative reasons a young woman might consider marrying a minister, perhaps subconsciously?
3. Are there any necessary character attributes one must have as a minister's wife? What might they be?
4. Must a minister's wife feel "called" to be one in order to function effectively?
5. Why or why not might it be dangerous for a relatively young Christian woman to marry a minister?
6. Can a marriage in which the minister's wife is more ambitious or capable than her husband be effective in church work? Why or why not?
7. Do you think a college education for the minister's wife is important? Why or why not?
8. Do you think a young woman's self-concept affects how she functions in her role as minister's wife? In what ways?

SUGGESTED READING

The Vision Splendid, "Relating," "For This Cause," by Dr. Paul Benjamin. (Deals with importance of the home front; its morale.)
Divorce in the Parsonage, "Introduction," "The Casualities," by Mary LaGrand Bouma. (Deals with ministerial pressures, dropouts, floundering marriages.)

21

2

YOUR PUBLIC IMAGE

"Mrs. Snodgrass . . . Hattie . . . I say, Hattie, I want you to meet our new minister's wife." (Now say hello to Mrs. Snodgrass, dear.) Charmingly you greet Mrs. Snodgrass who is perusing you from head to toe, wondering if you should do your tricks now or save them until you meet again. You feel she knows the brand name on your underwear, and can readily see on her face that her idea of a "minister's wife" is not quite coinciding with what she sees before her eyes! Tsk! Tsk! You grab your sense of humor for which you pray daily, and sail smoothly (we hope) through the interlude.

You won't be a minister's wife for very long without encountering something like that. If you're younger, it is even more difficult, because you still take yourself more seriously than is really healthy! It is said "life begins at forty," and I believe it! By then you have learned much from your mistakes, you know your own little foibles (which have been pointed out to you for some years now!), but you also know your strengths and have come to grips with yourself. You've been hanging around yourself so long and gotten to know her so well that you've actually begun to like her and think she's a swell ole gal after all!

Well, exactly what did you think Mrs. Snodgrass was looking for in a minister's wife? If she were meeting you at the community Woman's Club meeting, she would probably expect you to be a representative of your husband and your church. She thinks you know the times and places for all church functions. You have a "community reputation" to live up to. Naturally the local hospital guild sends you a whole packet of ice cream social tickets which you are to dispense to church ladies for a worthy cause. And it would be nice to lend your countenance (and name) to the Friends of the Library Committee, or please sign the petition to keep liquor out of restaurants on Sundays. If you could possibly join the community chorus (we sing the Messiah every year, you know), many ladies from your church may also come. This list is alternatively amusing, annoying and endless. But demands can be more serious too.

For instance, several years ago I received a phone call from the head nurse at the hospital. She was calling for my husband to come to help a woman threatening suicide. After explaining he was out of town, she asked for me to come and take care of the lady. They didn't know what to do with her at the hospital! Now if a trained nurse couldn't help in emotional problems, just what course in seminary was I to call upon for that? The point being that community people, and some church members as well, sometimes expect you to step in and act in place of the minister. I have even been asked by a county coroner to notify a woman of her husband's death (since my husband was out of town) before that same coroner contacted her about the situation. You may argue the point whether they should or should not expect us to step in for our husbands, but face the fact they do, and you may sometime have to deal with it. By the way, listening to and filling a person full of hot coffee (while praying fervently for husband to come home) does wonders in helping a person overcome suicidal tendencies! I wonder if they have that in the medical books yet?

What would Mrs. Snodgrass be expecting of you if she were a member of your congregation? Would it be the old stereotype of "silent partner" with your preacher-husband, dressed sedately (surely not in black?!), very discreet? You must, of course, be more spiritual, always volunteer to do good works, and know most (if not all) of the answers as to what's going on in the church. (Are church members really expecting that?)

In her book, *They Cry, Too*! (What You Always Wanted To Know About Your Minister But Didn't Know Whom To Ask), Lucille Lavender says, "A minister's wife should be attractive, but not too attractive; have nice clothes, but not too nice; have a nice basic hair do, but not too nice; be friendly, but not too friendly; be aggressive and greet everyone, especially visitors, but not too aggressive; intelligent, but not too intelligent; educated, but not too educated; down-to-earth, but not too much so; capable, but not too capable; charming, but not too charming."[1] In another book, *How to Be a Minister's Wife and Love It*, Alice Taylor says, "So much is expected of her—the health of an Amazon and the dedication of a Florence Nightingale, the patience of a Job and the zeal of a Carrie Nation, the peace-loving thought of a Ghandi and the fighting spirit of a warrior, the charm of a debutante and the intelligence of a Phi Beta Kappa. Besides this, she must live her life in a goldfish bowl, well aware that it is her sole responsibility to see that the goldfish behave.[2]

How much of this is truth and how much is fiction? What is the real feeling among churches today? According to the church survey, the following positive and negative traits in a minister's wife were listed by the congregations:

POSITIVE TRAITS: they want to see friendliness, genuine love and caring for church people; they want her to be herself (not act a role); they want her to love her husband and family; she should be patient, have a humble spirit, cooperate and be willing to work.

NEGATIVE TRAITS: they don't like to see unfriendliness, snobbishness, nor someone who is overbearing, critical, gossipy, withdrawn, inactive in church affairs, or who dominates her husband.

None of us can argue with the validity of these. In fact, they're right out of Galatians 6—the fruit of the Spirit for which every Christian should strive. Why then is there contention between the minister's wife and the church regarding expectations of her role? Can it be

1. Lucille Lavender, *They Cry Too* (New York: Hawthorne Books, 1976), p. 89.
2. Alice Taylor, *How to Be a Minister's Wife and Love It* (Grand Rapids: Zondervan Publishing House, 1968), p. 9.

25

what they expect us TO DO rather than what they expect us TO BE? In other words, our performance rather than our inward characteristics. Or is our communication with them so poor that what we think they expect of us isn't really what they expect at all? The survey among ministers' wives bears this out—many of us don't really know what is expected of us. The thing we do know is this: what we really are deep inside reflects what we do, or the spirit in which we do things. Perhaps there's error in both camps: congregations expect (sometimes unwittingly) unfair things of us, and we show our resentment by our lack of cooperation or belligerent attitudes. We are all (churches and individuals) in various stages of our Christian growth. None of us has yet arrived. Churches have personalities just as ministers' wives do. Some are pleasing, some are not. How a church accepts you as the minister's wife largely rests upon its former ministers' wives. Some will ascribe to you all the weak characteristics of your predecessors, especially if they've been the brunt of them. If one was bossy or dominated her husband, or gossiped, they will watch for just a spark of that in you. If one was well-loved, they will try to love you also. In essence, wherever you go you will be called upon to defend the title of "Minister's Wife," be it good or bad.

Some churches are steeped in tradition where the former minister's wife "always did this or that." That's fine. All traditions are not bad. Adhere to the good ones, but don't be afraid to forego the obsolete ones—with much tact, of course! Approach it as starting a new tradition!

Other churches may not have any traditions to break. Their attitudes reflect their locality, the types of people in the community, their vocations. For example, a church in a farming community in the midwest may differ in expectations from one in the industrial north. Some churches are known as "preacher killers"; on the other hand, some ministers are known as "church killers." The survey among ministers' wives bore out the fact that "nothing extra" was expected of ministers' wives in new church work, regardless of the area of the country. Traditions in these churches haven't had a chance yet to grow.

We need to start paying attention to the majority of church people who are "ministers' wife lovers," rather than the minority who are difficult to work with and prove to be the provokers. The latter have learned well that the squeaky wheel gets the oil. (But must they squeak so often?) In the applying of oil to these squeaky wheels we sometimes overlook the goodness and strength of the other good working parts (people). While we cannot ignore the pressures and stress involved in working with people, we can learn to set priorities and learn to keep them in perspective.

The following items of advice for ministers' wives was contributed by church members who participated in the survey:

- Not everyone will like you—don't feel offended. You can't please everybody.
- Some people put their mouths in motion before they put their brains in gear: be gentle with them.
- Don't expect others to be perfect; be patient.
- Most people in the congregation want to love you and be your friend.
- Take time out for yourself and your husband. Put him and your family before church work.
- Don't compare yourself with other ministers' wives—be yourself.
- When criticized, don't think everyone feels that way about you.
- Practice what you preach.
- Treat everyone equally.
- Leave home and family ties behind and get involved in the church where you are now.
- Love the people.
- Keep your priorities straight.
- Help, listen, support your husband in all he does.
- Don't be afraid to have friends and activities outside the church.

This advice sounds like good advice for any woman in the church to follow. Was it what you were expecting church members to say? It should be a real encouragement to you to see that the majority of church members are as concerned about your personal welfare as they are about theirs. They want you to be yourself, to be content and happy in your marriage and in your work. They also want to be loved and accepted by you. Therefore, take heart in the fact that the majority of the congregation feels this way, and try to keep the troublesome minority in proper perspective.

In summary then, be aware that people will expect different things of you, depending on their past experiences with preachers' wives, and depending upon their own church and cultural backgrounds. You do have a position of respect and leadership both in the community and in the church. Accept it with good grace and handle it wisely as a trust from God. The majority of His people love you and are out there rooting for you. Don't neglect to love and appreciate them in return.

REFLECTIONS

1. What particular expectations might a community have for a minister's wife? Is this true of your community?
2. Does your church expect the minister's wife to "fill in" for her husband? What circumstances may/may not be legitimate?
3. What nature of expectations seems to be the most demanding for the minister's wife—spiritual or physical? Why?
4. Which is more important to your church: the character of your minister's wife, or the activities in which she participates?
5. Is your church concerned about the outward appearance of its minister's wife or the house she lives in? Why or why not?
6. List some positive traits you feel are essential for a minister's wife to possess.
7. List some negative traits you feel are detrimental to her ministry (general).
8. Does your church have some unrealistic traditions for the minister's wife? If so, how can they be changed?
9. Do you consider yourself friend or foe of the minister's wife? In what ways do you express this?
10. What are some ways the minister's wife can be encouraged? Have you done any of these lately?

SUGGESTED READING

Divorce in the Parsonage, "Words to Seminarians and Pre-Sems," "Words to Wives and Girlfriends of Seminarians," by Mary LaGrand Bouma.

3

WILL THE REAL MINISTER'S WIFE PLEASE STAND UP?

Er . . . eh . . . Mrs. Preacher, is that you? Walk a little closer, will you, and look straight at me: I am your mirror! Stand up straight now and take a good look at yourself. What do you see? Sparkling eyes, a happy heart, a gracious lady? Are you a person at peace with yourself and those around you? Or do you see turned down lips, disappointment and discontentment on your face? Can you see right now what others see when they look at you, or are you busy playing the role of Minister's Wife? Are you free to be yourself, or are you hemmed in on every side by trying to fit into a mold you think others expect of you? Be honest now—no one's looking but you and God— what do you really see as you stand here before me? Whatever it is that you see or don't see, dear Minister's Wife, I hope the following chapter prompts you to examine yourself, your attitudes, and your "calling" as the minister's wife.

Your attitude about yourself will largely determine your attitude toward your ministry. If you feel inferior and inadequate as a person, it will be evident in how you function as a minister's wife. If you feel pressured into living up to or living down the reputation of a former minister's wife, that will affect your attitude. If you are at peace with yourself, know your weaknesses and strengths, yet feel God can help you make a significant contribution where you are, that will also be apparent in your attitude toward ministry.

Someone has said, "We are not what we think we are . . . we are not even what others think we are . . . we are what we think others think we are!" Are you letting others determine what you will be as yourself, the minister's wife? Are you so busy maintaining your defense that you have no time or energy to develop in areas of service which would stretch you and enhance your growing process? Can you honestly say you are the same person right now that you would be as a farmer's wife or a telephone lineman's wife? Are you a good worker in the church who just happens to be married to the minister? Have you let others push you into a mold, or are you free to be yourself to make your own choices of service, directed by the Holy Spirit— not the Women's Council?

Denise D. Turner whose husband is minister of religious education at First Baptist Church in Middleton, Ohio says she's hearing the rumblings of a liberation movement among minister's wives. She clarifies, "Well, it's not exactly a liberation movement. No one has burned a basic black dress or picketed a men's fellowship meeting. But numbers of ministers' wives are starting to claim the freedom to make choices, and they are not naive enough to sit around thinking someone else is going to claim that freedom for them. What is today's minister's wife clamoring to be freed from? Coercion for one thing— and sanctimonious labels and molds."[1] She goes on to enumerate what the minister's wife doesn't want: she doesn't want to be controlled by other people . . . she doesn't want to be labeled "super religious," and she doesn't want to be "the minister's wife." Now if Mrs. Turner perceives this to be a growing problem within the Baptist churches, is it just possible it is a problem within most other churches across our land? I am of the opinion that it is a widespread problem.

Over the past few years I have had a growing concern for the minister's wife and what appears to be an increasing problem with identity.

4. Denise D. Turner, "You Mean That's the Minister's Wife?" *Your Church,* Nov./Dec., 1979, pp. 42, 43.

There is an alarming rate of marriage problems and/or divorces among ministers and their wives. A growing number of them are leaving the ministry solely because they want to keep their marriages intact. This concern led me to conduct a nation-wide survey in 1982 among ministers' wives. I wanted to find out why they're having marriage problems and divorces, why they're leaving the ministry, where they hurt and why they're hurting, and what we can do about it. To give you a background of those who were surveyed, here is a mini profile of those who responded. Their suggestions, attitudes, and responses are recorded and utilized throughout the following chapters.

MINI PROFILE

AGE BRACKETS:
18% were 20 - 30 years old.
47% were 31 - 40 years old.
21% were 41 - 50 years old.
14% were 51 and older.

WORKING OUTSIDE THE HOME:
27% worked 30 or more hours a week (20% of these were in the 31-50 age bracket).
20% worked 10-25 hours a week (11% in the 31-50 age bracket).
50% did not work outside the home (with the exception of odd jobs).
94% of the workers did so for financial reasons (including children's education, clothing, and to help draw better Social Security).
52% worked because they "wanted to," "felt less depressed," it gave them "self-esteem and fulfillment," and for "social interaction."

COLLEGE EDUCATION:
80% attended a Bible seminary (38% received degrees).
12% received a secular degree (nursing, education).
8% did not attend college.

CHILDREN IN THE HOME:
65% had children in the home 0-12 years of age.
17% had children in the home 13-18 years of age.
9% had children away from home.

AVERAGE LENGTH OF MINISTRY:

26% under 3 years.
51% 4-8 years.
18% 9-15 years.
 5% 16 years and over.

TITHING:

100% believed in teaching it and practiced it.

MULTIPLE-MINISTRY:

45% have husbands who work in a multiple-ministry.
36% have husbands who do not work in a multiple-ministry.

RETREATS, SEMINARS, ETC.:

62% attend couples or singles retreats.
17% believe they're not helpful and do not attend.
21% attend sometimes; not a priority.

After studying the survey and talking to countless other ministers' wives, the greatest single need appears to be the same for the minister's wife as for any other wife—*the need to be loved for herself alone— not for whom she married or what she can do.* Many people in the church never get past the surface, hand-shaking-at-the-door relationship with the minister's wife. To them she remains just that. To some she is the associate minister who fills in when her husband is unable to do a job. She is asked to do so because of whom she married, not because of her capabilities. When she is continually robbed of her identity, the minister's wife will eventually suffer a crisis in self-esteem. When this becomes apparent to some church people, they wonder what's the matter with her. Why, surely being a minister's wife is no different than being a doctor's wife or that of some other professional person. I can't begin to count the number of times I've heard that sentiment. I do agree that the minister and the doctor both have impossible schedules to keep. Both deal with people, many times in stressful situations. However, there are some differences.

A minister has less freedom in accepted behavior than a doctor does. So long as the doctor performs well on the job, he is accepted regardless of any questionable weekend pursuits. Just let a minister even have the appearance of condoning or pursuing something questionable in the eyes of the beholder, and out of town on a rail he goes. His job is on the line by what he does with his "free time" (what is that?) as well as how he does his church work.

The doctor's wife does not usually choose her personal friends from her husband's clientele; the same set of people the doctor sees in his office are not usually the ones he associates with on weekends. The minister's wife usually associates with the very ones—problems and blessings—her husband works with all week. This is why making friendships is so difficult for her: the very ones she may be vulnerable with as friends are also ones who have the power to fire her husband!

The doctor is usually his own boss and can determine the hours he works, what days he can leave the office, and the length of time he will be gone—also his own salary. The minister has about 300 bosses (more or less) who tell him how to run his office practice, what to do with his time, how long he can be gone, and how much he can (or cannot) make. The doctor does "reasonably well" financially. His finances are usually ample enough to free him to leave town when the pressures are too great. The minister would welcome the chance to try living on the doctor's salary! Just think, no more worries over children's shoes, coats, extra school necessities, and saving for college education! And wouldn't it be a real blessing to have adequate finances that would free him to leave town for a few days when the pressures get too heavy; a sort of "emotional rescue" to save him from becoming a "Pastor Disaster" as one of my friends calls it. I've always wondered if the doctor's wife is asked to dispense medicine when her husband isn't available! Some ministers' wives have been asked to be "stand-ins" for their husbands as if they'd been through all the training and experience he has. As you can see, there are some distinct differences between the doctor's wife and the minister's wife. The minister is peculiar for a reason . . . he has a peculiar job!

There is much talk today about women and their fulfillment. The subject keeps nagging away at us via visiting ERA speakers, coverage in the newspapers, role models of the modern woman portrayed on TV, movies and magazines. Has any of this influence seeped into the church and caused the minister's wife to question her worth? Has she begun to measure herself by the world's standards rather than those found in the Scriptures? Is she seeking her identity in the wrong places?

And what about you, are you seeking identity in the wrong places? If you are seeking it in the role of Minister's Wife, you won't find it there—at least not enough to satisfy you. People and their expectations change, so your security in a role is too precarious. Better to find it in a personal relationship with God—He alone never changes. Nor can you find security in a person, such as your husband. It is not enough just to be his wife. We will all be called to give an individual accounting for the stewardship of our lives. You can't get to heaven on your husband's coattails and neither can I—no matter how good or how important we think they are.

The key to woman's identity lies in her love for Christ and his love for her. In *Women at the Crossroads*, Kari Malcolm says, "If women search for their identity in roles, they make idols of those roles, of their careers, their homes, their children or husbands. None of these things and none of these roles can give women what they are searching for. It is only on the narrow path up the mountain, only in a first love relationship with Jesus Christ that a woman will find what she seeks."[2] She goes on to say, "each time something replaces the love for Christ within us, inner conflict results. With this conflict comes a sense of failure and unfaithfulness to Jesus Christ and to ourselves, our dreams, and ideals. There follows a feeling of hopelessness and very low self-image." We cannot allow the world to influence us with counterfeit answers to our problems about identity. If we do, we're losing ourselves in the world, not in God. God has a lot to say about our worth. Did he send Jesus to earth for a "nobody"? Did Jesus come to die for a "nobody"? Was he victorious for a "nobody"? No! Thanks be to God we are His, we are loved, and we are Somebody!

> But you are a chosen race, a royal priesthood, a dedicated nation, and a people claimed by God for his own, to proclaim the triumphs of him who has called you out of darkness into his marvellous light. You are now the people of God, who once were not his people; outside his mercy once, you have now received his mercy (I Peter 2:9, NEB).

2. Kari Torjesen Malcolm *Women at the Crossroads* (Downers Grove, Ill.: InterVarsity Press, 1982), p. 23.

Mary Bouma, who wrote *Divorce in the Parsonage,* thinks the minister's wife falls into two basic traps:

1. THE SHEEP DOG SYNDROME: Here's where the minister's wife does all God, her husband, and the congregation want her to do. Unfortunately, these three things aren't always the same. "She's in an awkward position—neither pastor nor the sheep—she's the sheep dog running around in circles with her tongue hanging out, panting from exhaustion."3 Even though she works as hard as the minister she doesn't have the status, and she works as hard as other church workers, but isn't exactly "one of them." Is it any wonder she begins to feel resentment and frustration? Her husband does the exciting work and she's stuck with the busy work in the church nursery on Easter Sunday. If you are doing this, stop and ask yourself why. Do your gifts relate to these activities? Do you enjoy them or are they forced upon you? Is your family suffering because of them? Do you have the physical stamina for them?

2. THE COP OUT. This is the person who refuses to conform to the stereotype. She gets a job outside the home and is involved in the church as little as possible. Her husband was "called to ministry"— she was not. She has her own life to live. This woman is defensive and unhappy because her husband is disappointed in her; she feels cheated and guilty.

What is the alternative to these two extremes? Look up I Corinthians 12 and read about spiritual gifts. Aren't we one of many different parts of the body, none more or less important than the others—but all equally important to each other? Now turn to Romans 12. What does this say about using your gifts? We need to feel free to develop and use our gifts in ministry to Christ, offering leadership in these areas. Always be careful not to "think of yourself more highly than you ought to think" (don't hog the show, be a scene-stealer, a lime-light soaker), but rather train others. Your ministry will be enhanced and multiplied far beyond just what you could do alone. A word of caution here. Do not get so used to saying, "No, that's not my gift," that you pass up other opportunities to develop new gifts. For some

---

3. Mary LaGrand Bouma, *Divorce in the Parsonage* (Minneapolis: Bethany Fellowship, 1979), pp. 114, 115.

reason not many ministers' wives (or any other wives for that matter) have the "gift" of washing dishes in the church kitchen! Be careful that you're not just called to the highly-thought-of visible jobs that you miss the joy of meeting those delightfully humble women across the soapsuds in the kitchen. Jobs such as these are truly done out of love for Christ and others.

Some gifts we may have all our lives. Others we may have only for a season, corresponding with the changing seasons of our lives. When our children are small, we have special responsibilities to them. Most of our energies and gifts are used there in the home because children are time-consuming. When they are in school we have greater freedom for things outside the home. When they've finally left the nest, we have time on our hands. This is when we can really make a contribution (time-wise) to the work of the church.

At times we bring false guilt upon ourselves and sometimes others lay it upon us for something that really isn't our responsibility at all. Guilt may come from members who are still operating on their old stereotyped image of the minister's wife. Much we heap onto ourselves. We think we ought to do anything we're asked to do, regardless of our other responsibilities. We feel guilty that we're not perfect (or at least we don't live up to what we think they expect of us), so we try to overdo, to be "super pastors' wives," and end up being super disasters instead. These types of guilt feelings are illegitimate, so ignore them, and press on.

If you have feelings of inferiority (the root cause of lack of self-esteem), don't wallow in your own problems—look up beyond yourself and help someone else. James A. Dobson in *Hide or Seek* gives six (6) ways to cope with inferiority: withdrawing, fighting, clowning, denying reality, conforming and compensating.[4] Let me enlarge upon them and adapt them to our situations.

1. WITHDRAWING. This is the most common way of coping. If you surrender there's no chance or emotional risk of failing. You admit defeat and accept inferiority. This is also the fear of failure. The minister's wife who elects this way of coping is either misjudged

---

4. James A. Dobson, *Hide or Seek* (Old Tappan, N.J.: Fleming H. Revell Co., 1979), pp. 152-167.

to be stuck-up and snobbish, or because she seldom speaks, it is assumed she isn't thinking. Dobson says this group is a high risk for ulcers, migraine headaches, acute colitis, etc. Too much emotional tension is trapped inside.

2. FIGHTING. Have you ever seen a minister's wife with a chip on her shoulder? How much harm will this do the body of Christ if she chooses this way of coping with inferiority? No, it definitely will not solve the problem—but it will create more problems.

3. CLOWNING. This is the minister's wife who tries to laugh all those painful experiences off instead of crying over them. She gives the appearance of water running off a duck's back, when in reality it is sinking in and slowly killing her.

4. DENYING REALITY. This is a sad way to cope with inferiority. The person who chooses this way may drown her sorrows in alcohol or drug abuse. She refuses to believe she has a problem—that way she doesn't have to face it. Statistics are rising on housewives who are "closet alcoholics." I personally know of one minister's wife who fought this problem for over 25 years and died from it. There are no available statistics on ministers' wives who may have opted for this way out.

5. CONFORMING. These are the ones who turn into doormats and "yes-women." They're the bootlickers who toady to everyone. What a miserable life to be sure.

6. COMPENSATING. This is a process we use whereby we counterbalance our weaknesses by capitalizing on our strengths. We must be willing to change. For example, if 36% of the church people think it is helpful for the minister's wife to have musical ability (and they did in the church survey), but she has none, what shall she do? Perhaps she's a good seamstress or at relating well with people. She should seek to develop and use these talents to help build up the body of Christ, at the same time gaining self-esteem by being a person in her own right.

> Whatever gift each of you may have received, use it in service to one another, like good stewards dispensing the grace of God in its varied forms. Are you a speaker? Speak as if you uttered oracles of God. Do you give service? Give it as in the strength which God supplies. In all things so act that the glory may be God's through Jesus Christ;

to him belong glory and power for ever and ever. Amen. (I Peter 4:10, NEB).

We have a saying at our house that goes something like this: "You do what you can do . . . and that's all you can do!" Better yet, you do what you can do, then trust God with the rest. Our key to mental well-being is to accept what we cannot change. The "Serenity Prayer" says it well: "God grant me the serenity to accept the things I cannot change . . . the courage to change the things I can . . . and the wisdom to know the difference."

The best way of all to compensate is to lose yourself in service to Christ and to others. We need to cultivate the attitude of servanthood to which God calls all people, regardless of their roles in life.

> You know that in the world the recognized rulers lord it over their subjects, and their great men make them feel the weight of authority. That is not the way with you; among you, whoever wants to be great must be your servant, and whoever wants to be first must be the willing slave of all. For even the Son of man did not come to be served but to serve, and to give up his life as a ransom for many (Mark 10:42-45, NEB).

This servanthood Jesus taught by example (Luke 22:27; John 13:4, 5; Phil. 2:7). It should be based on love (John 14:14; 15:14) and brings happiness to those who live it (John 13:14-17; Matt. 11:28-30). Only those who have their self-esteem intact dare to admit their imperfections. But then, their acceptance isn't determined by what others think—their security is in God.

> For God himself has said, I will never leave you or desert you; and so we can take courage and say, "the Lord is my helper, I will not fear; what can man do to me?" (Heb. 13:6, NEB).

At one point in the Minister's Wife Survey which was noted earlier, they were asked, "How do you see your role as a minister's wife?" Here is how they responded:

67% think they should be good examples in all areas of life (trend-setters; support church programs).

33% see their role as teaching youth, leading women's groups.

12% do what their talents are: saying "no" to other things.

53% supporting their husbands, being good homemakers.
14% as an encourager, background worker, starting projects.
9% to have a personal relationship with God.
12% said they had no role.

It appears that "minister's wife" is just as hard to define as "mother" or "minister." Just as the role of the minister's wife can mean so many different things to each minister's wife, so expectations from church members can vary, depending on their backgrounds. For a young minister's wife, just reading this list will cause her stress level to accelerate at least 20 points! But take heart; being a good minister's wife is not so much in what all you can do, as much as what you are as a person. If you can keep in mind the following three words, it should be helpful to you. They are Attitude, Gratitude, and Latitude.

Attitude is what we must deal with first. Are we doing our service unto the Lord (Col. 3:23)? Do we love the church with a pure heart and want to do our best for the glory of God, not for the praise of men? Is our attitude one of servanthood? As the psalmist says, "Examine me, O God, and know my thoughts; test me, and understand my misgivings. Watch lest I follow any path that grieves thee; guide me in the ancient (everlasting) ways" (Ps. 139:23, 24, NEB).

Gratitude is an attitude we should build our lives on. Gratitude to Christ for the forgiveness He's brought to us, and for restoring us to Him, giving us dignity and worth. Gratitude that will spill out among the church people and community for a generosity which is prompted by God. Gratitude for the privilege of being a servant of God amongst other servants.

Latitude is a grace we must extend to the church to let them be what they are—and love them anyway. It is deferring one to another.

> Love in all sincerity, loathing evil and clinging to the good. Let love for our brotherhood breed warmth of mutual affection. Give pride of place to one another in esteem" (Rom. 12:9, 10, NEB).

There is a saying, "Be patient with me: God isn't finished with me yet." If you give people room to grow, there's a good chance you'll also be given some room to grow. Attitude . . . Gratitude . . . Latitude.

There are some very special rewards in store for the minister's wife, else celibacy among ministers would be running rampant for want of prospective wives! What other jobs offer a built-in acceptance in the church and community? You won't have to wait to be noticed, because you'll be asked about your gifts right away. You will be offered more opportunities to serve than you can handle. Living in your "glass house" also gives you an opportunity for service and for setting a family example. More people notice you because of who you are and who you live with. The church knows no cultural barriers. Just think of the many types of individuals with whom you come in contact, both in the community and the church—not to mention those traveling through who stop for a visit at the minister's house. But best of all is the opportunity to see individuals changed by the blood of Christ, to see them grow and mature in their faith, to share in their joys as well as sorrows. And the wonder of it all—God used you to do His work!

As you can see, a good deal of time was spent in this chapter, but a healthy self-esteem is one of the best foundations for coping with the title of "Minister's Wife." The world and the church are almost bursting at the seams with insecure people. How will you help them if you yourself do not have a good healthy self-esteem?

Now back away from the mirror, and get to work!

REFLECTIONS

1. What are some characteristics of a minister's wife who has a healthy self-esteem?
2. How can you tell when the minister's wife has made an idol of her role?
3. What might be some reasons that 50% of the ministers' wives feel a necessity to work outside the home?
4. What is the greatest single need a minister's wife has?
5. What do you think of the two basic traps Mary Bouma says preachers' wives fall into? Why do you agree/disagree?
6. In what ways may a minister's wife be (or feel) coerced by the church? How might this result in guilt on her part?
7. In what ways might a minister's wife exhibit feelings of inferiority? What are some specific ways of coping with these feelings?
8. What are some special rewards of being a minister's wife?

9. Is (or should) the gratitude of the minister's wife often expressed toward the church? Why/why not?
10. In what ways may a minister's wife show "latitude" toward the church?

SUGGESTED READING

Hide or Seek by Dr. James Dobson. (Deals with building self-esteem— not just in your children, but in yourself.)

The Vision Splendid, "Being," by Dr. Paul Benjamin.

Underground Manual for Ministers' Wives, "The True You," by Ruth Truman.

Read I Corinthians 12 & 13; Romans 12.

4

LIVING WITH THE PREACHER

"I Karen, take you Neil, to be my wedded husband; to have and to hold from this day forward: for better or worse, for richer or poorer, in sickness and health, to love and to cherish, til death do us part. . . ."

It has been almost twenty-one years since I first spoke these vows, little knowing then how much worse "worse" would get, how much poorer "poor" might get, and how much sicker "sick" would be!

Just how seriously do you regard your marriage? Is it a "til death do us part" commitment, or "til debts do us part" commitment? Is it "as long as you two shall live," or "as long as you two shall love"?

David and Vera Mace, who served seven years as directors of the American Association of Marriage Counselors, suggest the following as distinctive qualities in a Christian marriage in their book, *What's Happening to Clergy Marriages?*:[1]

---

1. David and Vera Mace, *What's Happening to Clergy Marriages?* (Nashville: Abingdon Press, 1980), pp. 24ff.

1. We believe that it was God who brought us together in the first place (the guiding hand of God).

2. We believe that our continuing life together is a part of the divine purpose. If we find and fulfill together our true vocations, happiness will be the inevitable rewards. We'll use our natural gifts and be service-oriented.

3. We believe that we have a witness to bear together; we will strive for growth in marriage relationships and be effective witnesses.

4. We believe that our shared life must have a sacrificial quality. We should live simply, frugally, with a comfortable standard, not as symbols of a rich society.

5. We believe that our Christian marriage must find spiritual expression. We want to share our feelings, experiences, Bible study and prayer.

Can any of us say our marriage is based upon these distinctive qualities? The Maces go on to enumerate these three essentials which they feel are necessary for a successful marriage: 1) a commitment to growth with a willingness to change, 2) an effective communication system (share your feelings), and 3) learning how to use conflict creatively. (The Maces have authored a book, *How to Have a Happy Marriage* dealing with this.)

Despite the high and holy ideals we all start out with, divorce in the ministry is rising at an alarming rate. One recent survey placed ministers in the third highest divorce rate by profession, just behind that of doctors and policemen. Note that these three are highly stressful, people-oriented professions. Why are clergy marriages falling apart? Are the minister and his wife competing against each other instead of complementing each other? Has selfishness seeped in from a "do-your-own-thing" society to threaten the marriages? Are our actions and decisions based upon feelings? Are clergy marriages threatened because of frustrations in trying to appease those with impossible demands in the church? Regardless of what truths may be found, it behooves us to really look at ourselves and the church, to ferret out those problems which are causing this rising number of clergy divorces, and which are making a mockery of marriage and teachings of the church. We have got to stop putting our heads in the sand, or piously saying we have no problems in our churches, when in fact we know of many clergy marriages which have failed, including some of the most well-known preachers.

In an article entitled, "The Divorce Dilemma," Larry Christenson suggests three warning lights that can help married couples steer through rough waters.[2] They are:

1. Silence (bottled up feelings). Take time to talk.
2. Sex (teach each other what is appropriate and enjoyable). Make an effort to keep this relationship vital and growing.
3. Separation (husband and wife go separate ways in work and activities). We need to spend time together.

In an article, "Notice the Divorced Among Us," George Ensworth says he considers marriages to be both a spiritual covenant before God and the church, and a civil contract before society. He says if we see marriage as a spiritual contract, wrongdoing isn't "limited to the overt sexual act with someone other than one's spouse. Rather, it may well be the infidelity of neglect and alienation because of one's preoccupation with a job or children or oneself. More often than not, these are the things that lie behind overt extramarital behavior, things that tempt a husband or wife to begin to look elsewhere for the understanding he or she perceives as missing in the marriage."[3] If we see marriage in this light, we realize there are more than just two people involved—there is also God as the third partner. Rather than placing the emphasis on a relationship, we place it on God. The promises we make to each other in our vows are on the basis of loving each other as we are—not what we want or expect each other to become. The promise we make to society is to live within the laws of the state. Our best friends, family and the church are usually there to set their seal of approval on this relationship.

In the ceremony we promise "before God and these witnesses to live together according to God's holy ordinances (laws)." We are aware that marriage is commended by God (Jer. 29:6); we know it is honorable in His sight, for Hebrews 13:4 reads:

---

2. "The Divorce Dilemma," a symposium with Larry and Nordis Christenson, Iverna Tompkins and Jamis Buckingham, *Logos Journal*, Nov./Dec., 1978.

3. George Ensworth, "Notice the Divorced Among Us," *Christianity Today*, May, 1982.

> Marriage is honorable; let us all keep it so, and the marriage-bond inviolate; for God's judgment will fall on fornicators and adulterers.

If then we make vows of marriage before God, dare we risk breaking them and having this judgment fall upon us?

God has much to say in the Scriptures about the obligations of marriage. (See Matt. 5:32; Rom. 7:2; I Cor. 7:10, 11). We had better not esteem his words lightly, no matter what social mores the world dictates. Mark 10:9 says, "What God has joined together, man must not separate." Christians live (or they should) by a different set of standards than the world does. Is it possible that we have allowed the world's standards to infiltrate the church, causing us to ask, "What is acceptable?", "What can I get by with?" rather than "What is right in the sight of God?" Read Matthew 5:31; 19:7; Luke 16:18 and I Corinthians 7:27 concerning divorce, marriage and adultery. How much can God bless us if we are unwilling to let him solve our differences in the marriage relationship? How can he restore us with his redeeming love if we have hardened hearts?

Ministers probably have to give up more than anyone else when they opt for divorce. Not only do they lose a home, a wife and children, but their jobs as well. How many churches do you know who want to hire a divorced minister? Undoubtedly his divorce harmed the church in which he was ministering at the time. His example and effectiveness were lost both in the church and in the community (as were the church's example and effectiveness). Some people will surely say, "Ha, all preachers are that way—nice sounding words, but they don't practice what they preach." For the Christian minister, or any Christian for that matter, divorce is not a good option. "For to love God is to keep his commands; and they are not burdensome, because every child of God is victor over the godless world" (I John 5:2-4, NEB). Marriages which are built upon Christ, not upon a relationship, will have a strong one-ness that will enable them to weather the storms. In marriages built upon Christ, the partners can be free to love each other just as they are; they will not have to compete with each other for acceptance. They can become good friends. If the husband is the head of the wife (Eph. 5:23), and the wife will in turn submit to her husband (Eph. 5:22), then the husband will be free to love her. He knows she will not take advantage of her strong influence over him. She will feel safe in submitting to him because he truly loves her and will not "lord" over her. Marriage becomes a duet instead of a duel.

Dr. Bruce R. Parmenter of the Christian Counseling Centers, Champaign, Illinois, says ministers' marriages may suffer from the kind of problems you see in other marriages, which include the following:

• poor bonding (the decision to marry was not fully and mutually voluntary)

• discrepancy in intimacy needs (intimacy is inclusive of sexuality but not limited to it—intimacy is the ability to be close in a variety of ways)

• power struggles (who is running the ship?)

• poor self-esteem

• unhealed trauma from the past

• immaturity

• value discrepancy

Wouldn't it be wonderful to think that living with the minister would be equivalent to living with a policeman or plumber or politician? But we know there are many important differences. Whereas the policeman, plumber or politician can leave his work when he comes home, the minister brings his along with him—it affects his marriage and his home. The whole family is involved in his job and they can either help him with it or prove to be a great burden. Ministers and their families do suffer from some stresses imposed upon them by the minister's professional role which, according to Dr. Parmenter, may include these:

• living in a fishbowl

• the minister is gone so much that his wife feels he is having an affair with the church

• ministers and their wives disciplining their children more severely out of their anxious need to be a model family

• the difficulty of being honestly human

• anxiety caused by certain troublesome church members.

The findings of Dr. Dallas E. Shafer, minister of the Christian Church of Security, Colorado in his DELPHI-80 project, bear this out as well.

47

He cites common factors in the breakdown of the minister's marriage to include disillusionment, loneliness and loss of identity. Results from the Minister's Wife Survey also bore out the fact that some wives are suffering from stresses imposed by their husbands' occupation. Following are some questions posed in the survey, and their responses.

- "Have the pressures of ministry ever been so great that you've encouraged your husband to seek employment in another line of work?" RESPONSE: 64% No; 36% Yes.

Comments they had written in included: "It would be nice to work for God for no pay" . . . "the blessings far outweigh the disappointments" . . . "why can't we have a sabbatical to refresh ourselves?" . . . "it's the man not the job that makes the difference."

Cited as reasons for encouraging their husbands to find a different type of job were: excessive complaints, criticism, endangered health, inadequate salaries, other interests and disappointment in local church leadership.

- "Do you consider marriage pressures a threat to your ministry?" RESPONSE: 70% No; 30% Yes.

Comments regarding this question were: "He takes it out on me and I have no where to go" . . . "pressures can cause us to be less effective" . . . "they brought us closer together" . . . "marital struggles are accepted, tolerated or seen with compassion in any field of work *except* ministry" . . . "we're afraid if people know we have problems they'll judge us unfit for ministry."

- "Have you considered a para-church ministry (counseling, nursing home administration, children's home, etc.) instead of the the local ministry?" RESPONSE: 32% Yes, at times; 68% No.

Comments they added: "they're all the pits, aren't they?" . . . "the pulpit ministry makes you vulnerable to the whims and hangups of people."

It is of little import whether you agree or disagree with these survey findings, nor whether you think stresses imposed upon the minister's wife by her husband's professional role are real or imagined. What does matter is that some ministers' wives actually are suffering from these stresses, as evidenced by their responses and that of their counselors. It is important for us to delve into the matter to expose the problems and find the solutions with a view to having emotionally healthy, happy and productive ministers' wives—a fact that greatly influences the health and influence of your own church.

But what about the "problem marriages" in the ministry? What of the domineering minister's wife who continually pushes her husband forward because "he doesn't assert himself enough"? She vowed to take him as he was, and now she vows to remake him into the mold *she* thinks a preacher should fill, if it kills him and her (and it may). She refuses to be under his authority; her lack of commitment to God (by refusing to do as he asks regarding the marriage state) slowly strangles her marriage and the repercussions spread out into the church. This type of woman is so eager to improve her husband's ministry (which of course reflects upon herself), and to correct his mistakes (which also reflect upon her choice of husband), that she takes the work of the Holy Spirit into her own hands to help "remake" her husband. It is not her job to correct or improve him, but she's impervious to this fact. He will deeply resent it if she tries to do so. It remains that work of the Holy Spirit. (See John 6:7, 8, 13.) If you have fallen into this trap, get yourself out of the way and let the Holy Spirit do his work. You'll be amazed at what God can do with your husband if you get out of the way!

Sometimes a minister will manage to marry an over-ambitious wife. She is more gifted than he, so she tries to make up for his deficiencies. She encourages her husband to try for positions in a larger church, or in the "glamorous" new church work, or in a missions endeavor where he will be highly visible in the brotherhood. This wife has learned well how to play church politics. She will help her husband get a position "worthy" of himself. (Which of course, looks good on her too!). She has a bad case of visions of grandeur.

Good marriages take time, energy, and work. They mean loyalty and commitment to each other and to God. They take time for communication, to play together, to pray together, and to study God's word together. They take submission to each other; they take sharing. In good marriages the husband and wife are careful not to defraud one another by over commitment—they have more than "left overs" to give each other.

49

The working wife may also cause stress on the minister's marriage. Of those who responded to the survey, 47% worked part or full time; 53% did not work outside the home with the exception of occasional jobs. 94% of those working cited financial reasons, because they "wanted to," or because it gave them "self-esteem and fulfillment."

Some ministers' wives are their own worst enemies. They get educated and introduced to the freedom of being on their own. They are trained for a vocation only to find themselves hampered by the demands of a marriage commitment. They become frustrated. They want the best of both worlds—the homemaker and the working woman. If either job is to be done well, the other one will suffer, so they're caught in the stalemate. The minister's wife may then embark upon the "superwoman" image—working two full-time jobs. How long will it last before demands of home and work make her choose one over the other, or bring her world tumbling down around her?

Some ministers prefer for their wives to work because of finances; some don't want their wives to work outside the home. The latter feel resentful and inadequate as a provider if their salaries cannot supply the needs of their families. Others will be resentful of the wife's job, for her working may be a statement that he can't quite support her in the style to which she feels entitled.

When a wife works outside the home, those from within the home have to "cover for her" while she's gone. It is obvious she can't do in the evening what is a full day's job, so some responsibilities must be meted out to others, and some must be left undone. If the husband is forced into doing home duties such as child-rearing, dishes, house-cleaning, laundry and meals, then his job with the church most assuredly will suffer. And so will her reputation within the church. It is evident that all must pay a certain price when the mother works outside the home. This is true whether the husband is a preacher, professor or postman. The minister's wife who is considering a job outside the home should ask herself these questions: "What are my needs?" "What are my priorities?" "Am I working for needs or wants?" "Am I pleasing my husband in this matter?" "Will the price I have to pay be too high?" "Are my priorities in proper order?" "What about the children?"

One of the greatest areas of contention which showed up in the survey was between the minister and his wife over his time usage—his priorities. Paul Benjamin writes "many ministers, however are not willful in their neglect of the homefront. Their families suffer primarily from default. . . . These ministers are keenly sensitive to the needs of their household. But like the politician and the business executive whose work has no perimeters the minister feels he never has any time left. He knows success is spelled W-O-R-K, but forgets Love is spelled T-I-M-E. . . . If the husband continues to put his work first year after year eventually even the best of wives will rebel. What is a minister to do when he discovers his wife is harboring a smouldering resentment toward him because of his neglect? If she does not revolt, often a state of chronic depression sets in. Her eyes grow sadder as the days go by. The atmosphere at home may be filled with either anger or despair. The children return home from school each day to a despondent household."[4] How will this depression and loneliness for companionship be resolved? Many have felt the demands were too high and have walked away from it all. Many have not walked away from it, but are suffering acutely from it.

The following questions in the Minister's Wife Survey dealt with this subject of time usage:

- "Do you feel your husband is 'married' to the church?"
  RESPONSE: 33% at times, 50% No; 17% Yes.

Some comments given: "Yes, I'm his concubine" . . . "No, you can avoid it if you want to—it's a matter of mixed priorities, especially with the younger minister."

- "Do you sometimes feel the needs of the minister's wife and children usually have to wait until everyone else's is taken care of?" RESPONSE: 45% sometimes; 32% Yes; 23% No.

Their comments: "There are certainly those times when I feel the children and I have to wait and some of our needs are not met by our father and husband, but I'm not so sure that this doesn't happen in other professions as well as ministry. It does create a situation where communication is vital. Sometimes as minister's wives we do not let our husbands know about our needs and *choose* to take second place. Usually this will not work forever as you reach the exploding point eventually where you end up a nag and he feels he is being put

---

4. Paul Benjamin, "For This Cause," *The Vision Splendid*, p. 1.

on a guilt trip." Yet other comments were a little more resentful than this one.

- "Have you ever been jealous of the amount of time your husband has spent with women of the congregation?" RESPONSE: 30% Yes; 70% No.

This was more of a problem for younger women in early marriage whose husbands counseled and transported young women to youth rallies and such functions. Some wives go along with their husbands for counseling, or the husband counsels in the home while the wife is present. Sometimes it isn't jealousy but irritation at the many demands and incessant calls to an "understanding preacher" who can't detect feminine wiles at work. A minister cannot be too careful when counseling women. He must be discreet and avoid situations in which either party might be tempted or compromised. He needs to jealously guard his reputation as well as that of his wife and the woman he is counseling. I Thessalonians 5:22 tells us to abstain from all *appearances* of evil. The key to dealing with this sensitive issue is trust and good communication between the minister's wife and her husband.

How the minister's wife regards her commitment to marriage will largely determine how tenaciously she goes about building her marriage relationship. If she regards it as a life commitment, she will have to creatively find a solution to the time-usage problem she faces with her husband. There again communication with him is a significant factor, along with an unselfish servant attitude on her part.

- "Has there ever been a time in your life in which your husband was gone so much that it left a void in your life and you were tempted to turn to an understanding male friend for help?" RESPONSE: 14% Yes; 75% no—a void, but no male friendship sought (11%).

Their comments: "I never turned to a male friend for I'm responsible to God for my thoughts as well as actions. I did feel like going away for awhile—visiting relatives, etc. I always tried to keep in mind each of us is responsible for her actions—we're accountable, so I never let the thought fester and take root."

- "What is the greatest cause of friction between you and your husband regarding ministry?" RESPONSE: 50% usage of time (no regular day off, home chores neglected); 14% there is no friction; 18% his handling of his job; 12% job stress and his health; 5% money problems; 6% his expectations for me.

Here are some of their comments on the minister's usage of time: "He's gone at nights when the kids are home and they're even lucky to see him on weekends" . . . "Some people seem to think the preacher's family has no needs or problems" . . . "Even our special days are taken from us" . . . "If I were sick I'd be on one of the preacher's rounds—if he had time" . . . "If this is a problem, it's the preacher's fault" . . . "Some preachers don't use common sense" . . . "I long for not just a day but a lifestyle of being able to escape from the demands. . . . I know it's the impossible dream, but can't help the desires of my heart!" . . . "The day after a second miscarriage he was called on his day off to come over to the church and clear the stage of chairs—it was one of my times of greatest need and chairs on the platform were more important."

The dialogue on usage of time between ministers and their wives will probably be here until the Lord returns. But when the husband or wife make value judgments for each other, there's bound to be friction. A wife may make up a "Honey-do list" (Honey do this, Honey do that) in an effort to control his schedule so there is time for her and the family. She may point out that the kids won't know who that man is sitting with Mom on graduation night. She may start addressing him as "Reverend," or write little notes on the back of the Roll Call cards with appalling messages. She may even refer to him as "what's his name" in an effort to get better acquainted! All these are signals that she is being neglected and needs a little time with the minister. Will he respond by examining his priorities and making time in his schedule for his wife and children, or will he ignore their needs by continuing his hectic pace? Perhaps he will retreat to the office to run away from the demands of his family. He may even resort to believing that old worn cliche that the husband is more spiritual and needs to be at his church work, while the wife (poor, emotional and practical creature that she is) must cope as best she can on the home front. This type of husband looks down his spiritual nose at his mundane wife as he does the "Lord's work" and leaves the "worldly" work to her. We all need to daily surrender our

53

egos to God so we may guard against hatred and bitterness, against spiritual snobbery and the martyr-complex which can be evidenced both in the home and in the church.

While we must cope with the negatives, we do not need to dwell upon them. So if you are full of worry, jealousy and discouragement, if you have a critical attitude and bitterness in your heart, if you are "angry" at the church for taking your husband's time. . . . STOP! You are trying to control your own life, not trusting God to take care of your needs and cares. You're letting the circumstances control you instead of letting God work through the circumstances to strengthen you. But there's good news for you:

> If we confess our sins, he is just, and may be trusted to forgive our sins and cleanse us from every kind of wrong; but if we say we have committed no sin, we make him out to be a liar, and then his word has no place in us (I John 1:9, NEB).

A few years ago I was in danger of coming down with the "mother-martyr" complex. Each wash day I would stand for hours (well, it seemed like hours) turning socks and underwear and shirts right side out. I pleaded, harrassed, harangued, cajoled, teased, and reasoned with my children and my husband, but to no avail. For some reason they couldn't remember to take off dirty clothes, leaving them right side out, thereby honoring me in my exalted position of wife and mother. Finally the Lord got through to me that I was measuring my self-esteem, and their regard for me by the wrong yardstick (or should I say underwear?). That year for his birthday my husband received one of the most costly and meaningful gifts I have ever given to him. It was just a simple envelope with a note inside which read: "Husband, I give to you underwear right side out (without complaint) for the rest of my life!" The surrendered ego is a costly, but necessary thing for peace in the parsonage or in any other home in our land.

Would that we could make our homes a haven of peace and rest— homes that provide warmth, privacy and a shelter (hide-away) from the excessive demands of our husbands' time and energy. Dear God, let the minister find a wife there who is affectionate and responsible, one who shares his burdens and ministers to the minister—one who wants to live in harmony as you intended.

Paul Tournier says "it is only when a husband and wife pray to-gether before God that they find the secret of true harmony: that the difference in their temperaments, their ideas, and their tastes enriches their home instead of endangering it. There will be no further question of one imposing his will on the other or of the other giving in for the sake of peace. Instead, they will together seek God's will which alone will ensure that each will be fully able to develop his personality. . . . Most of all, a couple rediscovers complete mutual confidence, because in meditation, in prayer together, they learn to become absolutely honest with each other. . . . This is the price to be paid if partners very different from each other are to combine their gifts instead of setting them against each other."[5]

REFLECTIONS

1. Do you agree/disagree with David and Vera Mace on the distinctive qualities a Christian marriage should have? In what ways?
2. To what do you attribute the alarming rise of clergy divorces?
3. Discuss the stresses on ministers and their wives cited by Dr. Bruce Parmenter. Do any of these stresses seem evident in the marriage of your minister and his wife?
4. In what ways might the minister's wife become disillusioned?
5. Are you surprised that 36% of the ministers' wives encouraged their husbands to seek employment outside of the ministry? Why do you think this is so?
6. What does it take to make a good marriage?
7. In what ways can a minister's wife working outside the home affect her husband's ministry? Enhance it?
8. What are some ways a minister's wife can deal with jealousy regarding her husband's relationships with other women in the church?
9. What is the greatest friction between the preacher and his wife regarding ministry? How can they cope with it?
10. How can a church encourage the minister and his wife in their marriage relationship?

5. Paul Tournier, "The Secret of Harmony," *Leadership,* Fall, 1981.

SUGGESTED READING

What's Happening to Clergy Marriages and How to Have a Happy Marriage, both by David & Vera Mace.

The Vision Splendid, "For This Cause," by Paul Benjamin.

"The Secret of Harmony," by Paul Tournier. *Leadership,* Fall, 1981.

You Can Be the Wife of a Happy Husband by Darien Cooper. (Wheaton: Victor Books, 1976). Deals with the link between a woman's true identity and God's role for her.

Divorce in the Parsonage by Mary LaGrand Bouma. (Why it happens and ways to prevent it.)

Spirit Controlled Temperament by Tim LaHaye. (Wheaton: Tyndale House) Deals with weaknesses and strengths in people.

5

GREAT EXPECTATIONS

According to the dictionary, "expectation" is defined as "assumption; act of looking forward to; to consider one is duty bound; anticipation of future good."

That definition encompasses both a positive and a negative attitude. For example, that of "duty bound" poses a negative part, while "anticipation of future good" is the positive aspect of expectation. Let us together explore both the positive and negative aspects of expectations in our ministry with the church.

How the minister's wife perceives the definition of her role, and what the church regards her role to be hold the keys toward whether their relationship will be that of adversary or friend. If there is friction in the relationship, what could have caused it? Did the minister's wife improperly assess the attitudes of the congregation in regard to her role? Do they really expect of her what she thinks they do, or is she jumping to conclusions? Remember the quote mentioned earlier, "We are not what we think we are . . . we are not even what others think we are . . . we are what we think others think we are"? This can be applied to the minister's wife in how she perceives her role for herself, and what she thinks the church expects of her. She may have built up unrealistic expectations for herself, and then feeling totally inadequate, placed the blame on the congregation for imagined demands on their part. She may have allowed a few of the discontent to influence her, and improperly conclude that the majority are dissatisfied with her. She may in fact, be fighting a "paper tiger" of her own making in regard to her role. Here again, how the minister's wife sees herself as a person directly affects her relationship with the church. Does she have a sense of self-worth? If so, it will be reflected in her relationship with the church. Does she know what her spiritual gifts are? If so, she will know where her best areas of influence lie.

According to the Minister's Wife Survey, 92% see their role as being that of home-maker, and a team worker (or supporter) with their husbands; 24% of the women see it as an opportunity for example and leadership among the youth and women of the congregation; 11% feel they should be friendly, helpful and encouraging to the women; 9% want to use their own special talents, not just "fill in" where no one else will work. I think this is a very commendable showing among them.

In regard to using their talents, 56% did not think they were imposed upon; 27% cited themselves as a problem in this area. They couldn't say "no," they took on too much because they enjoyed it—especially in the areas of church secretarial work and music; 8% felt they were kept from using their talents because of jealousy over ability, or because of their impermanent status ("This church is not your home, you're just a-passing through. . . .")

However we see ourselves as ministers' wives, we must bear in mind that Christ calls us all to be servants whether or not we are comfortable in that position, and whether or not the churches expect us to be servants. If Jesus, son of the Most High God could humble himself when He came to earth, taking the form of a servant (Phil. 2:7), and if He could perform the humble task of washing feet (John 13:14), and if he then charges us to be servants as he was (Matt. 20:28; Mark 10:43, 44), dare we stubbornly hold on to the false pride of thinking ourselves above others, to be "experts" or "professionals" hired to lead and tell others what they should do? I think not! We cannot even hope to be effective in ministry if our pride in position or selfishness regarding our own personal desires gets in the way of the humble servant attitude Christ calls us to have. Instead of selfishly seeking our own way, we must look for a larger picture of our effectiveness in the church, of which we are only one member of that body. Then we can look upon our roles afresh, and as Ecclesiastes 9:10 says,

"Whatever task lies to your hand, do it with all your might" (NEB). Instead of holding back to protect our interests and egos, let us put our whole hearts into our tasks and receive the joys of service awaiting us.

Not only is the relationship between congregation and minister's wife affected by how she sees herself, but it is also affected by how she sees the church, and by what she feels they expect from her. Below are some sources of friction which evidenced themselves in the survey. These sources were wide and varied, reflecting the different personalities both of the churches and the ministers' wives.

12% were bothered by unjust criticism of themselves, their husbands and children;

12% felt selfishness of people regarding time and demands on the minister's family;

6% were disillusioned with leadership in the church (lethargy, disorganization, failure to confront);

14% felt taken for granted; stifled; they couldn't be themselves;

8% felt most ladies' meetings were time-wasters;

8% were bothered by insufficient salary and parsonage needs;

12% were not sure of the friction, or had none.

Here are some more responses to what they thought church expectations were:

• "Does the church expect you to be a leader in the church?" RESPONSE: 47% Yes; 35% No; 14% no more than others; 6% Not sure.

Leadership areas in which they felt expected to lead were youth and women's Bible studies and meetings, teaching and example.

Responses from the survey indicated that the above areas of leadership were expected of the minister's wife nationwide, with the exception of the northeastern states: 73% there disagreed—the minister's wife was considered to be "one of them" in the church.

- "Does your church consider you to be working with them or for them?" RESPONSE: 12% felt they were working FOR them (highest in the Mid Central states); 67% felt they were working WITH them; 18% felt it was both ways (mostly in the South, Southeast).
- "Does the church think your husband's job is your job too?" RESPONSE: 18% Yes; 61% No; 21% Somewhat.
- "Do you think your husband's job is your job too?" RESPONSE: 45% Yes, we're a team; 55% No—we share and support each other, but each has his own responsibilities.
- "What does the church expect of you as the Minister's Wife?" RESPONSE: 23% No more than other leader's wives; 23% To support my husband at home and church; 38% A workhorse . . . super woman . . . assistant minister, attend every meeting, program; 8% They want to be proud of me; 17% To be friendly; 17% Nothing, I don't know.

The ministers' wives also had certain expectations for the churches and their leaders. Some were disillusioned with the leadership because of their lethargy, disorganization, and their lack of backbone, their lack of church discipline. Some concluded that when the church board majors in minors they are not very committed to the weightier matters of the church as they should be.

Prompted by their disappointment in the church, a minister and his wife may fall into the trap of thinking church people are "less spiritual" than they are, perhaps because they don't have a Bible college education. They may begin to regard church members as children instead of their equals—as brothers and sisters in the Lord—making themselves to be the "spiritual father and mother" in the church. This type of minister and wife may even begin to make decisions for the church people as their "spiritual leaders" which are not rightfully theirs to make, falsely thinking they can assume responsibility for another person's behavior. If you have become cynical in the ministry to this degree, it will be very hard to rid yourself of it. It colors your thinking in every area of life, eating away at you, robbing you of joy in the ministry, just as you are robbing them of their rightful responsibilities.

Discouragement can also come like a mighty blow when you discover a trusted member of the church board proves to be your worst enemy. It comes as a shock to you when he questions your integrity, your motives, after years of sharing in ministry with you. You are desolated to find he was subtly undermining your work all along. The devil seems to work overtime on ministers and their wives because of the great influence they have upon others. We dare not fall into the trap of blaming churches or individuals for our own disillusionment and cynicism. We alone choose whether discouragement in the ministry will be a stepping stone in our spiritual growth, or whether we will allow it to become a stumbling block. The Bible is full of examples of disillusioned people and how God helped them cope with it victoriously. It will help us overcome such disappointments if we will but go there for comfort and strength.

Some ministers and wives will themselves cause discouragement in the church. They begin to compare former ministries with their present one, either from the pulpit or the ladies' circle meetings. They put pressure on the church to produce like the last church did; or to have more elders and deacons; or to host some big, colossal, stupendous happening featuring the latest and greatest from Hollywood, Nashville, the Miss America Pagaent or the NFL, to so enhance their standing in the brotherhood or community. It is no wonder some churches become cynical about the minister and his wife. They don't like to be compared with other churches any more than ministers like to be compared with other former ministers. So if you're guilty of doing this, stop it for the sake of the kingdom.

> We should not dare to class ourselves or compare ourselves with any of those who put forward their own claims. What fools they are to measure themselves by themselves, to find in themselves their own standard of comparison! (See II Cor. 10:12ff.)

Stop right now and draw a line down the middle of a clean sheet of paper. On the left side write down all the things about being a minister's wife that you don't like. Go ahead and get it out of your system! Now look at this list and determine which things you can change for yourself—then cross those off. How many are left? Now list on the right side the benefits to you, your husband and your children that the ministry and church affords. Does it look more balanced than you thought at first? Now re-examine your feelings, your demands. Are they selfish or unselfish? Guard yourself that you don't get the "welfare mentality" in which you think the church must supply all things (Well, almost all—I've yet to hear of a church board offering free burial in the contract). Have you caught yourself wondering why Brother Spiffy hasn't offered you a discount at his clothing store, or why Brother Greens hasn't offered you a free pass to the golf links? Did you get aggravated when they didn't throw that annual birthday party for you, nor give you a Thanksgiving fruit basket? Are you looking forward to being sent off on a Holy Land Tour in honor of your outstanding service to them, and if they don't, will you become bitter and accuse them of being uncaring and parsimonious? If you are looking for extra benefits like the above, judging churches by their gifts or lack of gifts to you, you certainly might be rightfully accused of thinking of yourself more highly than you ought to think. There are many aunts and uncles, sisters and brothers, grandparents, mothers and fathers just awaiting us in the churches, if we will but look past our own selves to see them. Examine your true feelings; then stop being a self-seeker and be a soul-searcher instead. We need to realize that the majority of people are loving and caring people who want to work with us and help us belong. Don't try to measure their acceptance of you by how much they can give you.

One minister's wife wrote, "I have nothing but the utmost love and respect for the churches of our brotherhood. They are chocked full of godly loving people. They are trying to cope with this accelerated life style and the clever deceit of the Devil just like all the rest of us. They certainly don't need to be 'put down' nor blamed for the pressures in the parsonage that they also feel and deal with in their own homes."

If you are looking for gossipers, slanderers, back-biters, the critical and the moody, they'll all be there in the church. If you are looking for the friendly, the caring, the working, the Christ-filled and the loving, you'll find them there also. You will find exactly what you're looking for in a congregation, with a few surprises thrown in to make life exciting! In the vernacular, "what you see is what you get," or what you are looking for is what you'll find, and what you probably wanted to find.

At times ministers get very frustrated because they're unable to carry out some much-needed programs. They have people who are trained, but can't get motivated, and people who are motivated, but can't get trained. A very small few who are both motivated and trained—may their tribe increase! In order to get things moving some ministers assume the title of "Director in Charge" of everything. These may be the ones who regard church people as children, and make decisions for the church body "for their own good." They write the checks, appoint the elders and deacons, and are a rule unto themselves. They assume the end justifies the means. But does it? Can they justify denying others with hidden potential the opportunity of developing and growing in leadership? When the minister leaves that church, will it fold up because it was all built upon a person (minister) instead of THE person—God? Will the church flounder for years until someone comes who will allow the natural leadership to come to the fore, to be encouraged and trained for service? Undoubtedly so. What is the glory then, if all their work is gone when they leave that congregation because they ran the whole show? Selfishness ("I'm more qualified, better educated than they are") kept them from being a wise steward of their time in regard to equipping the saints in that church. Pride which prompts them to do it all so it'll look good in the community and the brotherhood also keeps them from wise stewardship in equipping the saints. Where there was one minister, there could have been many. Guard with all your might against these attitudes. If pursued they will encourage laziness among church members or develop a clergy-laity mind-set in which the clergy are paid to do the work and the laity sit in the pew and dare anyone to motivate them. A passive religion. It certainly will rob church members of their rightful service to God. It will steal their joy of being on the growing edge of the church.

I am concerned over a growing attitude of "reverse snobbery" which is creeping into some churches today. Churches which harbor this attitude welcome to their bosom the poor, underclassed, physically disabled, sin-laden persons into their midst—and I praise God for that. They feel sorry for people who are not as well off as they are.

They fall in love with the person who continually says "woe is me, I am nothing." However, they have great difficulty in loving the confident Christian who is at ease before the crowd, the one who sings or speaks well. They are very good at "weeping with those who weep," but very poor at "rejoicing with those who rejoice." People who appear in various stages of slouchy dress (down home clothes) and appearance are welcome. Those who appear in their "Sunday best" are not perceived to be honoring God with their best, but judged to be snobbish, appearing better than the others. People who sing special music in these churches may do so well that they are accused of singing with their noses in the air, or thinking they're better than the rest. Choir members might feel intimidated when a "good voice" joins the choir and threaten to leave the choir if the "good voice" doesn't excuse himself and leave first. A church with such tendencies might profit from a choir member like the one in this ditty. (It fits the tune of "Up on the Housetop.")

> Up in the choir loft there I'll be; I love to sing of his love for me.
> But I don't need to follow our director dear—For I know it by heart
> and can sing by ear!
>
> Ho, ho, ho—I don't know; Ho, ho, ho why they stare at me so;
> When they asked me to sing they had no fear—
> How were they to know I had a "tin ear"?!

I am reminded of an occasion where several ladies had gathered to discuss and plan an area ladies' retreat. They were discussing ways of getting more ladies from the local church involved in the planning and attendance. One lady remarked, "Well, I didn't come last year, because I just thought it was the preacher's wife's idea!" Now that lady said a mouthful! In that congregation many women had bad feelings for a former minister's wife who was evidently very visible in leadership roles in the church—which fact they resented. This same congregation did not want the minister's wife to stand at the back door greeting people as they left church, for that would be "putting on airs" . . . trying to act important. This congregation needed a minister's wife who was willing to do much work, but get no credit; one who would encourage and train some natural leaders, but would keep a low profile. It takes years for old suspicions and hurts to be healed over. These people needed to be loved into finding their own gifts for service, and then encouraged to use them. Perhaps you are ministering in a church such as this. Try to help them gain a sense of their own worth and self-esteem. Believe in them, and encourage them to tackle something harder. Be willing to do things out of the limelight as well as in the limelight. I'm concerned with the attitude some ministers' wives have who only want to do "my own things . . . my own talent." Can this be interpreted "what *I* want to do"? We must continue to develop ourselves in new areas, the humble tasks along with the glorious ones. We cannot expect someone in the church to do something we would not do ourselves. They must learn by our attitudes and actions. It's like the kids say: "Talk is cheap." It's the servant attitude again, which God calls us all to have, regardless of whether or not others around us will.

A growing frustration among many ministers' wives is the amount of demands being put upon their time. Forty-five percent felt that their time was being monopolized by church members. Expectations were that they attend every church function, class social, ladies' meeting, be able to give a devotional or teach a lesson at a moment's notice or to fill in in absentia for their husbands, attend all church weddings and personal showers, baby showers, rehearsal dinners and weddings, and the list goes on. In fact, many ministers' wives have resorted to working outside the home. Not only did it help monetarily, but it gave them an excuse for not attending daytime functions, and for saying "no" to evening functions in the church. Many ministers' wives are expected to be walking computers. They should know all church data past, present and future. The person who invents a computer to hold nursery schedules, names of church and class officers, sick people in the hospital and nursing homes, identity of all on the church role, times of all church activities, and instant devotional thoughts is going to make a mint in the ministers' wives market!

The frustrations that come over expectations for us to attend all of these "worthy" meetings are especially felt in the 20-40 age group where there are small children in the home. By the time the children are grown, the minister's wife has matured enough to feel confident about her role and can say "no" when reason demands it. The older minister's wife doesn't feel she has to prove herself. She has become accustomed to the position she has undertaken. She has also had a chance to develop a sense of humor in dealing with the many demands upon her time.

Another time-consuming area for the minister's wife is the telephone. If her husband isn't home to receive a call, she may get the joy of being the listening ear. This can save the minister some precious study time, and hopefully save him from that dreaded operation she had feared (telephone-removal from ear). Counseling either on your husband's behalf or your own can be very demanding. Sometimes the minister's wife is sought out because of her position; she is neutral, unbiased, unprejudiced (we hope). When someone confides in you, learn to keep your mouth shut. Don't betray confidences or your effectiveness will be lost.

There were 82% of the ministers' wives in the Survey who were sought out for counseling at least one to three hours per week; 18% were not. Most wives felt inadequate and unprepared for this. It would be helpful for Bible seminaries to offer at least a basic counseling course for the prospective minister's wife which deals with general counseling, and some crises handling for the terminally ill, "death calls," and etc.

In the end we must learn to set some limits for ourselves and keep them. We must let them be known to the congregation too, not expect them to learn by osmosis. If you set limits and tactfully make them known, most people will stay within them and respect you for setting them. ". . . in all things so act that the glory may be God's through Jesus Christ; to him belong glory and power for ever and ever. Amen" (I Peter 4:11, NEB).

The problems of certain expectations and identity will be with us in every church. For if the churches continue growing, new people will be joining the fellowship, bringing with them their preconceived ideas from various backgrounds. If our members remained the same, and if we remained in the same church, we could eventually train people to accept what we want our roles to be. But we will not always remain in one place, and hopefully the church will continue to grow. In some churches former ministers' wives may or may not have had the same role concept you do. The ones following you may think differently too. This could also account for the mixed attitudes in the church regarding their expectations for you. It is unprofitable for us to spell out a certain role definition for the minister's wife. It would not contribute toward harmony in the church nor be profitable to attempt to train the church to accept a certain policy toward their ministers' wives. Rather it is a matter of attitude on the part of the church as well as the minister's wife. With each new minister's wife will come a new relationship to be nourished and cultivated by both the church and the minister's wife. There has to be good communication if they are going to work in harmony. The reason most people don't think like a minister's wife is because they've never been one. They will only be aware of some of her problems if she is willing to share them at some time. There must be a give and take from both viewpoints. A church can't expect a paragon of a woman and a human being at the same time; neither can a minister's wife use her role only when it's convenient for her, then discard it when it is not quite so convenient. She has to come to some kind of acceptance of her role, to realize that with position comes responsibility.

If you are fighting your role and certain expectations the church has for you, why not stop responding negatively? Instead respond positively by asking yourself, "How can God use me in this unique situation in this unique place to minister in a way in which no one else can?" Ask yourself if you truly have the servant attitude of Jesus. Accept your lot and be content in whatever state you find yourself. If you will accept the church with her banes and blessings, that attitude will likely rub off in their regard for you as well. Then both the minister's wife and the church will be allowed some "growing room" in which they can blossom and grow together as they labor for their mutual good.

The Apostle Peter sums it up well when he says,

> Be one in thought and feeling, all of you; be full of brotherly affection, kindly and humble-minded; Do not repay wrong with wrong, or abuse with abuse; on the contrary, retaliate with blessing, for a blessing is the inheritance to which you yourselves have been called (I Peter 3:8, 9, NEB).

REFLECTIONS

1. Do most ministers' wives really know what is expected of them? Why/why not?
2. Why do you think some ministers' wives are defensive in their roles?
3. Is it possible for a quiet, withdrawn minister's wife to be effective in enhancing her husband's ministry? What about one with an outgoing personality? Why/why not?
4. Why are some ministers' wives disillusioned with the ministry?
5. Discuss the pros and cons of the style of ministry in which the preacher functions as a "corporate chairman of the board." Is this biblically sound? Does it affect the minister's wife any?
6. Enumerate some things ministers' wives may expect of churches.
7. What are some symptoms of "reverse snobbery" which might be found in churches (or ministers' wives) today? Are any of these symptoms in your church?
8. How can a minister's wife deal with demands upon her time for the mutual benefit of all concerned?
9. Should churches spell out a certain role definition for the minister's wife? Why or why not?
10. What are some positive ways a minister's wife might respond to church expectations?

SUGGESTED READING

Be All You Can Be by David Augsburger. (Carol Stream: Creation House, 1970).

My Utmost for His Highest by Oswald Chambers (New York: Dodd, Mead & Co., 1935, 1963). Excellent devotional reading for motivation.

6

DEALING WITH CRITICISM

One of the most painful and difficult things to deal with as a minister's wife is that of criticism. At some time (or many times) in your life as the minister's wife, you will be the object of criticism. How will you handle it? Will you immediately be defensive and counter-attack, or will you withdraw and simmer until you're a boiling cauldron inside—with a good case of ulcers thrown in for good measure? Will it totally cripple your self-esteem, or will you be able to survive the debacle and build upon your experiences?

Look at the Person (Critic)

There are many reasons why people criticize. It may be that the minister's wife has made a mistake, or appears to have. Perhaps criticism was given in the heat of anger, or as a bid for your attention. Maybe you are not living up to their expectations in your role. There may be some stress in the life of the critic unrelated to you, and you are just the target for misplaced anger. Some people feel a sense of power when they can vent their anger on someone of "position." It is important for us to learn to assess or evaluate others—to ask, "Why are they saying this?" Paul Benjamin says, "Figuring people out is not necessarily cruel and unchristian; it is absolutely essential if we continue to minister effectively. Otherwise we are always at the mercy of those who keep causing mischief because we fail to see through their schemes. Being naive is never listed as a Biblical virtue."[1]

Criticism can be used by manipulators. They will choose a time and place in which many can be witnesses to your hopefully emotional demise. They seek to discredit you before others so their power can be enhanced, or their esteem raised, whereas the person who is truly upset with your behavior, but caring as a person, will approach you privately.

The most difficult ones to work with are those who lack a healthy self-esteem. They are insecure themselves and resent those who appear well-adjusted. These people indulge in back-handed compliments, such as "You did a much better job of singing than the last time you were up there." The implied criticism of the last time is an effort to get you to doubt yourself. They want you to know they know others much more proficient than you are—you don't quite measure up.

Criticism can also come from another person on the church staff who suffers from insecurity. There may be intense competition and jealousy, or backbiting in an effort to jockey for power and acceptance above another on the staff. These people do not make good team workers. In a situation such as this, the problem becomes much more complicated to deal with, because you are being shot at from all sides. Even your "own kind" are taking potshots against you, undermining and hurting your ministry. They have violated the charge in Philippians 2 of esteeming others better than themselves.

Then there are the destructive church members. As Paul Benjamin writes, they "may represent only a very small percentage of the total membership. Still, we must be consciously aware of their power. Alert leaders must take whatever steps are necessary in order to limit their influence. Many destructive people have no honor. They will stoop to any level—even lies and hate mail—if a power struggle in that church comes to a showdown."[2]

1. Paul Benjamin, "Dealing with Difficult People," *The Vision Splendid,* p. 64.
2. Ibid., p. 68.

An excellent example of this is the letter printed below. It was written to a young minister's wife who is also a dear friend of mine, and was largely responsible for provoking me to attempt this book.

Dear Mrs. Preacher's Wife,

Well, I am glad you finally came home, and hope that you had a Merry Christmas with your daddy, and spending money that I had to sacrifice to give you. I cannot believe that our church board let you leave and be away from your job on the most important religious holiday (Christmas), not to mention they gave you an advance on your pay. What a spoiled brat. When my husband and I get to travel (which isn't often) we have to plan ahead and save our money, but not the preacher and his wife. We really feel that your husband could do a tremendous job with the young people if you weren't always hanging around and running your big mouth—and I do mean big. We finally got our high school kids to church for the Christmas season and thought at last maybe they could meet you and your husband and spend some time with them, only to find that you had left town. Great—in the past they were always involved in things for the kids, but for some reason they won't come any more, and I guess no one cares because your husband hasn't even bothered to call. But then I know he has to take good care of you. I wonder who will be more important at the gate of heaven. I know that you are pregnant, but do you know that you are not the only woman to ever be pregnant? I mean after all, I am sick of it! No one else ever had to ask for prayers from the whole congregation just because they were gonna have a kid. Take it from me, Mrs. (Preacher's Wife), the people in this church are sick of you and your big mouth, sick of hearing you sing every other time we go to church, sick of you being such a big fake, and such a big baby, sick of you putting down your husband in front of others. Why don't you stay home where a good wife belongs and let your husband be the minister? I think he is the one I voted for when you came. Believe me, you are running the whole show. If the elders don't stop you soon, there won't be any youth for your husband to work with. (The Senior Minister's wife) could probably give you a few pointers on staying home and being crafty, so you won't have to be your husband's shadow. I know times are hard and I am probably feeling sorry for myself, but you make me and a lot of other women at the church SICK . . . GROW UP AND SHUT UP YOUR BIG MOUTH. God can hear you and I don't want to.

I wish I had the nerve to talk to you, but then you would only hate me and my kids both, so pray for my kids on New Year's Eve because I know they won't come to your party because of your uncouth and crude manners. I'll be praying that you will stay home just like other wives have to do, and not run our husband's business. Also, while I am getting this off my chest, you need to know that there are a lot of people that feel this way. It isn't just me and my family. But we are all afraid to tell anyone about it, so think about it and every time you scream that big mouth of yours, think of me; every time you have to stay home alone while your husband is working, think of me and the other wives who cannot run their husband's business; think of me every time someone sings in church. Remember that several of us are glad it's not you; think of me, but most of all, when the kids get in trouble on New Year's Eve, and should be at the church party, think of you, as you regularly do.

"A mother who is worried"

P.S.: Tell your husband we think HE is doing an Okay job.

How did you feel after reading a letter like that? Since I know the young woman who received this quite well, I can tell you there aren't any "grains of truth" to be found here. The only one that could possibly be considered is her "joy de'vivre"—she enters the room hilariously happy. What do you suppose she felt? God help us all to minister to these women who have been wounded so deeply by wicked letters such as the above, so we don't lose them from the ministry because they feel unfit after so much criticism, or just can't take the abuse any longer.

Some of you may have already received "hate mail" such as this. Examine it. Did the critic seek to attack the behavior of the person or the person herself? Was it meant to change the situation or destroy the person? It is so important when criticism comes that we learn to be objective. Learn to evaluate—first look at the critic.

How can your words be good when you yourselves are evil? For the words that the mouth utters come from the overflowing of the heart (Matt. 12:34, 35, NEB).

Look at the Criticism

After you have tried to objectively look at the critic, then consider what has been said. Is there a particle of truth in the criticism? Was it meant to damage your personal esteem? Does it reflect jealousy or resentment on the part of the critic? Were your actions misunderstood? Did you actually give offense? What exactly was the aim of the criticism? Carefully weigh the criticism to see if it is just nit-picking harassment, or if it has some credibility. Is criticism of you being used to undermine your husband's effectiveness? We cannot afford to take criticism at face value, but must look below the surface for the truth. (See Prov. 18:17.) Some criticism can be handled carefully at the scene of the crime, while very hurtful criticism needs a cool head and a prayerful heart to successfully combat.

> To draw back from a dispute is honorable: it is the fool who bares his teeth (Prov. 20:3, NEB).

What about "constructive criticism"? The biggest percentage of criticism leveled at ministers' wives is not meant to be constructive. Although we can grow from it, the motive of the critic is not one aimed at our personal growth. It is meant to destroy self-esteem, not to build it up. Criticism breaks down a trusted relationship, and erects protective walls. Although this type of criticism is not constructive, how we perceive it can be.

An example of this is Joseph and his brothers. Jealousy and envy of Joseph's position, bitterness and criticism on the part of his brothers caused him to be sold into slavery and cut off as dead from the rest of the family. Those brothers still get credit for what harm they did, even though we understand their motives. Yet, at the big moment of revenge, Joseph's attitude changed the whole situation, even though he knew their evil motives. He had the perspective to see how God could take something evil and bring good from it, regardless of the intent of the brothers. God can still do that with us today if our hearts are right.

There is a type of criticism which is necessary in all areas of our lives. You may call it admonishment, reproof or correction. The Bible gives us some definite guidelines (Gal. 6 and Matt. 18) in both the giving and receiving of correction. These guidelines deal with motives and the methods of reproving. In the *Christian Standard*, Opal Lincoln Gee recently wrote, "Criticism that we must give can build or destroy. If we correct in a spirit of compassion, following the Bible's pattern, the beauty of discipline is honored in our homes, our work, and the church.

"As we receive criticism we must also weigh it in the balances of love. If we overreact to false accusations against ourselves and permit them to destroy our self-esteem, it serves Satan. However, when we allow corrections to shape us into the best we can become, the very image of Christ, it becomes wonderfully creative."[3]

My grandmother was great for walking into the middle of an apparent crisis and would calmly say, "This too shall pass." Although annoying at the time, it is absolutely true! Step back and gain a better perspective. As my dad says, "Ten years from now, will it make any difference?"

Charles Spurgeon once said, "Get a friend to tell you your faults, or better still, welcome an enemy who will watch you keenly and sting you savagely. What a blessing such an irritating critic will be to a wise man. What an intolerable nuisance to a fool!"

Almost half of the ministers' wives in the survey responded to criticism of their husbands angrily, defensively, and with much hurt. When criticized personally, most of them were "hurt and upset." About 30% had learned to cool down and think it over before confronting the critic. They seemed to have done better coping with personal criticism, than criticism toward their husbands. There needs to be a warning here, that we should not take up another person's offense (husbands, in this case). God gives us sufficient grace to handle the wrongs against ourselves.

Some ministers' wives in the survey wrote in these comments: "This is probably the hardest area for me and I believe for most wives who love their husbands, know how hard they work and try to live 24 hours a day what they preach. I'm afraid my tendency was to defend him, when I would have been better off to have kept quiet" . . . "It seems to me we need to renew and refresh and strengthen our relationship with the Lord. We need some remedial work in that area. If we are to keep our minds constantly on things of God (Phil. 4:8)

---

3. Opal Lincoln Gee, "Creative Criticism," *Christian Standard,* May 1, 1983, p. 9.

trivial things fall into place" . . . "We need to listen, let it hurt, dump it if not true, change if it is, try to forget it, and pray for self and critic."

Look at Yourself

After you have tried to assess the motive of your critic and have examined what was actually said, then take a look at yourself. Were your motives pure? Do you have mannerisms or habits that are offensive? Do you always have to have your own way? Could it have been a personality clash? Was this criticism a valid assessment of your actions, or a judgment of your self? Were they making a value judgment without having all the facts, or misinterpreting your motives? Were you overbearing or super-pious? Were you trying to provoke criticism consciously or unconsciously?

There are many ways we can bring criticism upon ourselves, and we need to analyze the situation to see if we are at fault. Sometimes we have to live with mistakes and poor judgments made in time of crises. Sometimes there is poor communication which results in misunderstandings and disagreements. If so, rectify what you can, and let the rest lie in the past. But learn from the situation so you won't have to repeat the same mistake twice.

In Matthew 7 we're told to take the beam from our own eyes before attempting to remove splinters from our brother's eyes, and in I Timothy 4 we're admonished to take heed unto ourselves. So examine yourself. Are you just as guilty of criticizing another minister's style or content of sermons at the last church convention? Do you harbor professional jealousy over another brother who brags of the way he "runs" his church? Or of a sister who brags about how highly her church women speak of her? Do you have impossible expectations for some church leaders and their families, and talk about them to others when they don't measure up? Do you strike back when attacked? Do you get involved in church controversies and then are offended when criticized for it? (See II Tim. 2:23.) If so, why not repent, ask God's forgiveness and start all over again with a pure heart. Then say with David,

Create in me a clean heart, O God; and renew a right spirit within me (Ps. 51:10).

If then, there is some truth in the criticism, seek to change the error of your ways. The rest that is not true throw away along with any guilt feelings the unjust criticism might have produced. If the critic is one whom you know to have emotional problems, then "you strong bear with the failings of the weak" (Rom. 15:1). You may not be able to control their conduct, but you can control your attitude toward them.

Learn to be tactful and gracious, and also to be a good listener. Control your tongue (See Prov. 25:8; James 3:13—4:12); keep from retaliation (Rom. 12:17), and pray for those who despitefully use you (Matt. 5:42-48).

A wise man (or woman) who speaks his mind calmly is more to be heeded than a commander shouting orders among fools (Eccl. 9:17).

Oswald Chambers has written, "It is not so true that prayer changes things, as that prayer changes me and I change things. God has so constituted things that prayer on the basis of redemption alters the way in which a man looks at things. Prayer is not a question of altering things externally, but of working wonders in a man's disposition."

Only those who have their self-esteem intact dare to admit their own imperfections: their security is in God. Don't let criticism destroy your usefulness in the Kingdom.

Let us even exult in our present sufferings, because we know that suffering trains us to endure, and endurance brings proof that we have stood the test, and this proof is the ground of hope (Rom. 5:4, 5, NEB).

REFLECTIONS

1. When the minister's wife is confronted with criticism, what is the first thing she should do?
2. What might be some possible motives for criticism?
3. If you had been the recipient of this anonymous letter, how would you have responded?
4. Is there such a thing as "constructive criticism"? Why or why not?
5. Is there a type of "criticism" which is necessary to us all? If so, what?

6. Why do you think it is easier for the minister's wife to cope with personal criticism, than that toward her husband?
7. When faced with criticism, what three things are good to keep in mind?
8. If criticism against us is valid, what should we do?
9. If criticism against us is not valid, what steps should we take?

SUGGESTED READING

The Vision Splendid, "Dealing With Difficult People," by Dr. Paul Benjamin.

Potshots at the Preacher, "Criticism and the Preacher's Wife," by James Allen Sparks. (Nashville: Abingdon Press, 1977).

"Creative Criticism," *The Christian Standard* by Opal Lincoln Gee, May 1, 1983.

Be All You Can Be, "Can You Be Your Best When Mistreated?" "Can You Be Your Best in Forgiveness?" by David Augsburger (Carol Stream: Creation House, 1970).

7

TIME FOR THE FAMILY

Not only are there peculiar pressures put upon the minister's wife, but there are some special pressures put upon his children as well. Parsonage parents are concerned about their children's "image" or "performance." They know that if their children get out of line there will be lasting repercussions on their ministry in that congregation.

To be sure, there are certain hazzards for the minister's children. Church people may have a certain set of rules for them, formed by their own personal feelings. They seem to have a list of things that minister's children aren't supposed to do. Some of them will condition the minister's children to expect goodies (like gum, candy, money, etc.), then criticize them if they ask for more. When the children are small they get carted and carried, teased and taunted, but they are not "allowed" to fight back. One of the biggest hazards these kids face is that they're not given enough room to fail, to make mistakes as other children are bound to do. It is natural for these children to fight this double standard of behavior. Wouldn't you, and don't you as an adult?

We as parents, need to teach our children that security doesn't rest in living by a certain set of rules someone else thought up for them, or in a house they don't own, or how long they stay in a certain church or community. Rather we need to teach it and live it that security comes from their (and our) relationship with God and our family. If we are resentful and rebellious over an unfair set of rules for ourselves and our children, then they will be too. If we express how much joy and how rewarding it is to live in the parsonage (despite the unrealistic expectations and demands imposed upon us by some), chances are our children will come to love it too, and be able to cope with it. Children usually reflect their parents' attitudes, no matter what house they live in.

Somewhere I read that statistics reveal more people listed in "Who's Who" come from homes of ministers, than from any other profession! Can it be they got a head start in dealing with people as they were growing up in the parsonage, or the fact that many people expected them to be leaders and achievers, so they believed they could and did? It behooves all of us to help these minister's children turn the stress of that role into a positive, growing, maturing experience. Let's teach them the little niceties of proper phone manners, how to meet people and how to develop a sense of humor. Let's not dwell on the negatives for ourselves or our children; let's dwell on the positives and possibilities of what we might become.

The minister's children need to be "fathered" like all other kids need to be. When they are robbed of his time (either by himself or church members), and of his attention, they will complain, or rebel, or eventually learn to get along without him. Most churches have their share of ministers' kids who have left the faith because Dad was so busy "saving" everyone else's kids that he had no time for his own. The case is similar to the cobbler's kids who had no shoes. Since the minister's kids are his nearest "congregation," he dare not neglect them for someone else. They are indeed his "churchwork" just as his wife is. When the stakes are so high, dare he risk them all in his quest for a "successful" ministry?

James Dobson thinks the biggest obstacle facing the family today is overcommitment—time pressures. He says, "There is nothing that will destroy family life more insidiously than hectic schedules and busy lives, where spouses are too exhausted to communicate, too worn out to have sex, too fatigued to talk to the kids. That frantic lifestyle is just as destructive as one involving outbroken sin. If Satan can't make you sin, he'll make you busy, and that's just about the same thing."[1]

Few ministers neglect their families on purpose. It happens slowly, and ministry becomes a 24-hour job. We've all heard "it's the quality of time I spend, not the quantity." I am reminded of the story about the young newly-engaged seminarian who said this to his sweet little bashful girlfriend: "Honey, I love you so much, that I'll give you 20 whole minutes a week of my time—just for you!" Ah, yes, lucky her! She should invite him to leave, after which he could pick himself up and dust himself off! You can just bet your kids won't fall for that line either. While they're growing up, quantity of time is important too. Don't let your child feel he has to compete with God and the church for the attention that is his due, and which he needs desperately. Sometimes it isn't a question of quantity of time, it's a question of availability at the time of need.

Some ministers are guilty of taking "family time" and using it for themselves. They may satisfy their own needs for a diversion and rest, but the family is cheated of time with Dad. This is why a wife occasionally becomes jealous of a golfball or a ballgame or a tennis racket! These objects have taken precedence over her. The minister must learn to take time off for himself, as well as—but not to the exclusion of—his wife and children. The gamble not to do so is too great. The health of his marriage and the affection of his children are at stake.

Did you ever meet a minister who was about as easy to pry away from his job as it is to pull hen's teeth? (You say you married him?!) This minister doesn't realize he threatens the security of his wife by not giving her a priority with his time. She needs to feel she is worth more than a "Hello-goodbye-Kiss-My-Foot" relationship. She isn't really looking forward to an early widowhood brought about because her husband has killed himself with his overcommitment.

---

1. James A. Dobson, (interview), "Snatching the Family From Its Grave," *Christianity Today,* May, 1982.

Once when our girls were smaller we had planned a special outing just for our family. It was planned far in advance, and we all eagerly awaited the big day. As so often happens in the ministry, a crisis arose and one of the elderly church members passed away. The girls were in tears, and one of them wailed, "but somebody *always* dies on Daddy's day off!" It is true priorities must be taught, disappointments have to be dealt with, and we must learn to be flexible. But it is also imperative to schedule or reschedule them when necessary, because we'll never get the time off together if we don't.

These last few paragraphs have been hard on dear old Dad, but what about Mother? Is her schedule as inflexible as her husband's with overcommitment of time? Does she feel like she has to be involved in every church function that comes along, whether or not she needs to be? Does she have too much work or so many interests outside the home that the kids are growing up by themselves or raised by babysitters? Are they virtually without father and mother, until bedtime? The question remains to be asked: "If you're too busy for them now, will they be too busy for you someday?" Are you really being good stewards of your children's lives?

Is There Time for the Relatives?

Perhaps this thought has never crossed your mind before. If you are in an area close to your relatives, they may at times demand too much of you (in regard to time—family birthdays, dinners, reunions, etc.) because they have no concept of a minister's priorities or schedule. Maybe your family isn't close to each other, and when you left home there wasn't much of a relationship to sever. Are any of us guilty of cultivating a relationship with all but our relatives? You know, the ones that aren't quite in our league. When there is a family crisis do we minister as a caring part of that family, or do we let "the preacher there" do it? Sometimes we do better for casual friends than for our own families.

When my husband and I were first married, the thing we fought over most was relatives! You know, the kind of attitude of "I like your mother-in-law better than mine, Honey." If my family was criticized I would ruffle up like an old turkey and vociferously protest. Why?

Because they were a part of me, so I myself was being criticized. Perhaps the fact that they are not esteemed as highly as they should be by some, has something to do with the difficulty of winning those in our own families. Are we too busy "saving souls" to comfort those of our own earthly families when it is within our hands to do so? We surely should not jump at their every whim, but we should not neglect them either. Since I came from a very closely knit family and had lived in one place all my life, marrying a preacher was a hard step to take. I knew I could no longer be a part of the frequent family get-togethers, and would be kind of "on the fringe" of the fellowship. I have never regretted the choice, but none-the-less, have felt the loss. When you try to be open to the leading of the Holy Spirit, you can't exactly expect God to settle you within driving distance of your family!

Just recently we received word of the death of my cousin from a construction accident. The following evening the phone rang again. This time, one of my nephews had fallen onto an electrical line and was badly burned. They knew his arm could not be saved, and his life was hanging in the balance. In two days our fall revival was to begin, and we had several obligations for the coming week. How could we possibly get away to go and be with the family? We prayed into the night, and in the morning my husband made the decision to fly back home with me to be with our family. He went as a husband and family member, not as a minister. In that single act I knew without a doubt that he loved me for who I was, and chose to put people ahead of church programs. What a blessing those actions were both to me and my family. They knew the choice he made indicated they were indeed very special to him. He's learned about priorities.

In *Killing Giants, Pulling Thorns,* Charles Swindoll says, "Busyness rapes relationship. It substitutes shallow frenzy for deep friendship. It promises satisfying dreams but delivers hollow nightmares. It feeds the ego but starves the inner man. It fills a calendar but fractures a family. It cultivates a program but plows under priorities."[2] He goes on to give this advice about time management:

ADMIT IT—openly; STOP IT—say "no," correct your priorities; MAINTAIN IT—invest time with family while you have them; SHARE IT—share benefits with others of putting first things first. You'll be more effective because of it.

1. Charles R. Swindoll, *Killing Giants, Pulling Thorns* (Portland: Multnomah Press, pp. 78, 79.

Stop and examine yourself. Are you investing enough time with those who matter the most? Is your hectic schedule robbing time from your husband and children? Does your frantic busyness defraud your partner of a physical relationship, your fatigue stifling communication of any kind? Are you allowing overcommitments, busyness, and fatigue to insidiously destroy your marriage and your home?

Old habits die hard, so early in life you must choose a life pattern with proper priorities, for they'll probably remain with you all through your ministry. And if you're older, it's never too late to start. It is never too late to start doing something right. God honors obedience at any age.

> Therefore to him (or her) that knows to do good, and does it not, to him (or her) it is sin (James 4:17).

REFLECTIONS

1. Why is it not unusual to hear of a "preacher's kid" who has turned completely against the standards from which he was reared?
2. What are some hazards ministers' children sometimes have to face?
3. What are some unusual benefits ministers' children may have?
4. What needs of a minister's family are sometimes jeopardized by the minister's overcommitment?
5. What needs to take place before a minister and his family can come to agreement over his time usage?
6. Do you think it is generally true that ministers exhibit more concern toward their church members than toward their family members? Why/why not?
7. On the other hand, do you think some ministers may use the excuse of care for relatives that they rule out God's leading in places of service? Why/why not?
8. Parsonage families seem to experience friction mostly in regard to the minister's usage of time. Why should that be so?

SUGGESTED READING

Hide or Seek, "Coping Can Be Catching," by Dr. James Dobson. *Divorce in the Parsonage,* "The Walking Wounded: Wives," "The

Walking Wounded: Children,'' by Mary LaGrand Bouma.
The Care & Feeding of Ministers, "The Eighty-Hour Week Made Easy,'' by Kathleen Nyberg.
The Vision Splendid, "For This Cause,'' by Dr. Paul Benjamin.

8

TIME OUT

In this day as never before the minister is beset with every kind of project or "good works" by the church family or community. They see him as one who has much influence over many people—a key person—and clamor for his attention and participation. Committee chairmen know that if the minister will just put in an appearance or give some input, the program is on its way.

If the minister is conscientious about sermon and lesson preparations, he will have some self-imposed demands upon his own time. He won't be satisfied with regurgitating back a sermon book outline, but will want to do some additional study on his own. How then will he fit in yet another demand upon his time?

Church members who belong to community service clubs would like for the minister and his wife to join their clubs, and be a positive influence for the community, or at least be their guest speaker for some occasions. The community ministerial association, area ministers' meetings, camp board, area men's fellowship and many other organizations are all looking to the minister for his support and participation.

In the midst of all these expectations stands the minister's family. The children want Dad to watch them play ball or take them to school events, or just be at home to spend time with them. The wife would like to have him home for family time too, if only for the psychological unloading of complete responsibility for the children from her shoulders. And, oh yes, it'd be fun just to be alone for one evening without any interruptions to have a real conversation and see what color his eyes are again!

It is at this point that the minister has to realize if he is going to participate in any of the above, he must learn to choose proper priorities. Notice I didn't say "priorities," but "proper priorities." The schedules we all keep reveal very well what we deem the most important. What we leave for last signifies the value we really put on it. Perhaps we have fallen into the trap of letting our schedules control us, rather than the other way around.

Results from the Minister's Wife Survey show that the greatest friction between ministers and their wives related to his usage of time: 79% noted this problem. There were 15% who listed time frictions between them and the church to be the greatest cause.

It is clear the minister's wife blames her husband for his time priorities (79% did), rather than the congregation (15% did). Their sources of friction with the congregation were: the constant phone ringing mostly for unimportant matters, selfish demands for their husbands to be everywhere at every meeting, expectancy to jump at command, demands on their own time to attend every church function, ladies' meetings, all personal wedding and baby showers of members and/or their relatives.

Their sources of friction on time management between them and their husbands were over his refusal or failure to take a regular day off, failure to spend some nights at home while the children were there, and help in putting them to bed, failure to spend time just with the wives, and failure to take care of needed house repairs and yard chores.

Many women (50%) felt their husbands were or at times were "married to the church"; 77% felt the needs of the minister's wife and children were or sometimes were left until everyone else was cared for; 36% had encouraged their husbands to seek employment in another line of work because of job pressures; and 30% have been jealous of the amount of time their husbands spent with women of the congregation; 75% experienced a void at his absence and 14% sought, or were tempted to seek, an understanding male friend for help in loneliness.

Are the churches actually demanding this time sacrifice or is it self-imposed by the minister? The Church Survey shows that 96% of the church people thought the minister should definitely take a regular day off and that church members should respect his need to do so. Well, if the church members expect the minister to take time off, and the wife wants him to, who needs to make the decision that determines it? You're right: #1 Husband!

If you are honest with yourself you'll admit to reasoning with him, expressing concern for his health, fear that the children are being neglected and cheated of a father's influence and all that good kind of stuff. If that doesn't work, you'll probably try arguing, cajoling, demanding, accusing and NAGGING. But if you're like me, you'll also have to admit that it hasn't helped all that much. Maybe he'll apply band-aid treatment for a few weeks or so, but then it's back to business as usual. You hope the squeaky wheel (that's you!) will get some oil, but he runs the other direction to escape the nagging and continues what he's already chosen to do. From the looks of the Minister's Wife Survey, this battle over time is still raging. Are there any quick fixits or easy solutions to this ever-growing problem? Probably not.

The minister's wife cannot make priority decisions for her husband (much as she would like to) or advise him on making them. The Holy Spirit has to do the convicting or he will never be able to set priorities and keep them.

This problem is similar to that of being the wife of a cigarette smoker. She can lecture him on the health hazards, grab the cigarette from his mouth each time he lights one up, harp incessantly, line up possible husband prospects at the event of his demise, or install smoke detectors, all to no avail. He can kick the habit only if he has an inward desire and motivation to do so—and most of all, with God's help.

The minister has to be convicted of the need to rearrange his priorities by the Holy Spirit. When a wife questions her husband's usage of time, he will immediately perceive it to be an attempt to grasp his authority (decision-making) away from him. Most men have an inborn

89

tendency to not "boss" well, and we can thank the Lord for that! But what in the world are we going to do with them?

Understand Him

Your husband may be one who has an insecure ego, and is pushing and driving himself unmercifully to succeed, thus trying to build himself up through praise and recognition from the church. The criticism you give him over his time usage is just another blow to his self-esteem. Or your husband may be in the middle of a demanding church building program, or at the beginning of a new ministry which will demand more of his time than usual. Your added pressure will only bring more stress to an already stressful time. Be patient with him.

Love Him Unconditionally

Let him know you love him just as he is. Don't try to remake him to fit your standards. Be the best cheerleader he has, so that hopefully he will regain his sense of worth from the value you place on him as a husband, and will not have to seek it through being a workaholic. Love him for the way he loves the church and has given his life in service for it when he could live with much more financial security in another line of work. Love him for the way he cares about people and their needs. Let him know your love doesn't hinge on whether or not he chooses what you want him to do.

Get Your Own Heart Right

Examine your own motives to see if you are being immature or too demanding—selfish. Do you resent being the only one who changes dirty diapers or scrubs floors? Do you want to have the same freedoms he does, or the freedoms you had before a husband and family obligations came along? You did say "I do," didn't you? Do you realize where you are today is directly related to a series of choices *you* made?

You have heard "two minuses don't make a plus." Well, two tired people don't make for understanding either. Even if you can't coax your husband to get his needed rest, you can determine whether or not you will get yours. You also have to set your own priorities. Are you gone practically day and night for church and community functions, or for things you like to do? I believe "as goes the mother, so goes the home." Determine to be rested so you can deflect those short, curt responses from a tired husband. Spend some special time each day in Scripture and in prayer. Hide God's word in your heart to keep from sinning (Ps. 119:11).

Make your home a safe and happy place to be so he can hardly wait to get there. It may take a little candlelight, soft music and home-made bread, but it's well worth the effort!

Communicate

Communication without condemnation has to be the plan here. Your man is under tremendous pressure to produce both in the church and in the community. If he is in his 30's he is in the super-conscientious period of his life. He may be pushing himself to his limit. More and more ministers are suffering from mental problems and burn-out. They're changing vocations and even changing wives because of the tremendous amount of stress upon them in the ministry. They are in desperate need to draw apart to a lonely place for a much-needed rest, just as Jesus called the disciples to do (Mark 6:31). You need to carefully communicate your fears, anxieties and frustrations to your husband in such a manner that you are not accusing him of neglect, or trying to produce guilt in him. Do so prayerfully, then wait for results. Hold him up before God, not only as he makes a decision, but at all times.

> And we know that all things work together for good to them that love God, to them who are the called according ot his purpose (Rom. 8:28, KJV).

REFLECTIONS

1. When ministers have difficulty controlling their schedules, might the concept of their role of ministry have any bearing upon it? Why or why not?
2. What's the difference between controlling your schedule and letting your schedule control you? What can be done to achieve control over it?

3. What do you think of the survey results regarding friction between the minister and his wife over time usage?
4. What steps can be taken to alleviate this friction over the minister's time usage? . . . by the minister?
5. What steps can be taken by the wife to alleviate this friction?
6. What steps can be taken by the church to alleviate this friction?

SUGGESTED READING

Hide or Seek, "Coping Can Be Catching," by Dr. James Dobson.
You Can Be the Wife of a Happy Husband, "Accepting Your Husband As He Is," "Helping Your Husband Love Himself," by Darien Cooper. (Wheaton: Victor Books)
How to Be a Minister's Wife & Love It, "All Work and No Play Make for Dullness," by Alice Taylor.

9

TIME OUT FOR . . .
RETREATS, CONVENTIONS, SEMINARS

The value of attending retreats, seminars and conventions should be evident to every minister and his wife. It is certainly evident to those church members surveyed because 92% thought the minister and his wife should be financially encouraged to attend these gatherings to better equip themselves for ministry. They know that a rested, refreshed, encouraged and renewed minister and minister's wife will directly affect the life of the congregation.

These activities we should not try to do without. If we constantly "give out" in church work, but never take in, we become stale and stagnant, or discouraged and disheartened. It's a place for fresh ideas, fellowship, encouragement, new insights and fired up enthusiasm.

It is good to know ministers' wives have a healthy attitude regarding seminars and retreats. Of those surveyed, 65% attend when they can; 15% rarely do so, and 20% do not attend at all. These latter two groups cited the following reasons for not attending:

"I didn't enjoy them" . . . "They were not helpful" . . . "Most workshops for ministers' wives are always the same" . . . "There were few opportunities" . . . "No babysitters to leave children with."

One minister's wife was bothered by some attitudes she encountered at retreats. She felt the only time she sensed being put on a pedestal or set apart from her sisters in Christ was not at the local church, but when ministers' wives got together at retreats. Others felt ministers' wives could be a great support group, but waste time "puffing up their egos over numbers and successes, and ignore the pain in the parsonage. They often are too holy to admit hurt and thus become patronizing." One wife wrote, "What has torn me up at retreats is the self-righteous attitudes of the preachers' wives themselves who are too insecure (or whatever) to admit that they experience the loneliness . . . that we surely all face."

The tendency in some retreats seems to be a glossing over of the strains and stresses—ignoring the negatives, instead of dealing with them for positive results. These negatives are swept under the carpet, with only joys and blessings to be mentioned, which are self-evident. They are why many choose to enter the ministry in the first place. Glossing over negative aspects of ministry does a great harm to those who attend such functions looking for an understanding shoulder to cry on, ideas for coping, encouragement to keep on keeping on, or just to escape the pressures at home for a short time. What better place to look for understanding, help and encouragement than a group of ministers' wives who have experienced the same stresses and are hopefully coping with them successfully? Instead of listening and encouraging the younger and/or hurting ones to talk out their troubles and gently guide them, there are some older ministers' wives who say, "Buck up, girl and get ahold of yourself; if you're having trouble it's obviously a personal spiritual problem." No, we need older women who are willing to be painfully transparent and honest about their past experiences in ministry—not super pious model role-playing. What seems trivia at 50 can be very traumatic at 25, and we seem to forget that.

A few ministers' wives who participated in the survey chided me for asking questions about the negative side of ministry. They wanted to talk about the joys and blessings instead. Opinions were expressed that younger wives were acting like babies, crying over their stresses of the ministry. While this may be true of a few who have been economically and emotionally spoiled in their childhood, I don't believe it to be representative of most of them. They earnestly have a desire to serve the Lord, and have chosen the ministry in a time when the profession is not nearly so highly revered by people in general as it was some twenty or thirty years ago. Since then the Watergate mentality has even hit the church and it's open season all year round for the minister and his family in some churches.

Perhaps we're expecting the younger ones to have the spiritual and emotional maturity and insight it has taken us years to obtain. Perhaps we are unconsciously jealous that they don't have to put up with what we had to do over the years. We do them a great disservice when we present only the pollyanna platitudes of ministry. We actually insult their intelligence when we sweep under the rug all the actual stresses that have to be dealt with. Many a starry-eyed idealist minister's wife has been cut off at the knees because she wasn't given adequate preparatory armor for the fray.

If we truly desire to keep these younger ones (and not so young ones) in the ministry, and to achieve harmony in our churches between the minister's wife and the congregation, we will have to unbend as older ministers' wives. We are going to have to tell it like it is, talking about the negatives of ministry as well as the positives. We will have to be transparent and honest with them. Only then will we be free to minister effectively to them. Retreats offering a balanced view of the ministry and how to cope with it is a good place to start.

REFLECTIONS

1. In what ways can a church encourage the minister and his wife to attend ministry-related seminars, retreats, etc.?
2. What are some reasons a minister and his wife might not avail themselves of these ministry-related helps?
3. Were you surprised about the attitudes between some older and younger ministers' wives which surfaced in the survey? Why or why not?
4. What might be some reasons for resentment between older and younger ministers' wives?
5. What can be done to alleviate the negative feelings which exist between some older and younger ministers' wives?

6. Do you agree/disagree that most ministers' wives' retreats, seminars, workshops, etc., are not too helpful? Why/why not?
7. What suggestions do you have which might improve the effectiveness of seminars, retreats, workshops, for the minister's wife?
8. Try to relay above suggestions (from #7) to the proper channels so ministry to these women can be more effective.

10

FRIENDSHIPS IN THE LOCAL CHURCH

One of the heaviest burdens the minister's wife faces today is loneliness. She has only her husband to share her troubles with, and sometimes she cannot do this without burdening him more. Many books for ministers' wives on the market today have fallen into two camps of thinking on this subject: the dare nots (you must not, cannot, dare not have personal friends in the local church), and the defiants (I can and I will have personal friends no matter what happens). The case against friendships cites these reasons:

- You might choose unwisely and she'll (your friend) use your confidences against you—you're too vulnerable;
- When you leave this church you will continue your friendships, and it's not fair to your successor;
- You can't impersonally "pastor" your friends because you don't see their faults;
- Others may become jealous and harm your ministry;
- It may expose your friends as targets for jealousy;

• Your personal friends may become jealous for your time, demanding and expecting special favors—manipulation.

A tidy list, to be sure. And what alternatives do these advocates offer to meet our needs for personal friendships? They suggest we make friends with ministers of another faith in the community, or friends in the business community who have other fields and interests different from ours.

Of those ministers' wives surveyed, 55% felt free to form intimate friendships in the local church; 45% did not; 5% weren't sure. The age group 51 and older felt freer to make friends (60% yes; 40% no); the group 31-40 were more cautious (39% yes; 61% no). The youngest age groups (20-30) agreed 57%. Many of this latter age group were wives of associates who felt having more than one minister's wife on the staff shielded them from much of the criticism. There were more than one minister's wife to draw the fire of criticism, so it was not as intense.

Believe it or not, the Church Survey revealed that the majority of church people expect the minister's wife to have personal friends. 70% of them felt it was a good thing for her to have personal friendships; 30% did not think they should, and 5% felt they should have something more than a casual relationship, but not a personal one.

Ministers' wives need to be encouraged by their congregations to form close friendships in the local church. Too many seem to have been hurt from such relationships and are afraid to risk it again, thus curbing some very natural and necessary emotional feelings.

I personally think the minister's wife should form intimate friendships among the church women. I am too empty and lonely without them. This is one thing that bothers me most at the change in place of ministry. No one can (or no wise one would) just move into a new community and grab up a few close friends in the church right away. One must start all over again to develop friendships. They take time to grow. It also takes quite awhile to discover one you can completely trust. You must choose with great caution and care; "put them through their traces" if you will, to see if they can keep confidences, and love you for who you are, not for whom you married, or for what you can do for them. Some people will shy away from the minister's wife when they hear who she is. They have a certain role expectation for her. They feel stifled when she's near because they don't know what to say. Their feelings inhibit a close relationship and promote loneliness for the minister's wife. The Book records that Jesus dared to have a closer relationship with Peter, James and John from the chosen twelve. If he had this need and did not suppress it, do you think He requires something different from you? His risk was that someone would let him down (and Peter certainly did), but that did not stop him from cultivating that close relationship.

If you choose to develop close friendships, be careful not to flaunt them at church; be discreet and do not be cliquish. If you spend special time with a close friend during the week, why not keep your time open for others at church gatherings? It will protect both yourself and your friends from criticism. A wise woman will avoid close friendships with those of the opposite sex in order to steer away from temptation and malicious gossip. Loving will make us vulnerable, but it's the only way to live fully.

In the long run it is best to find close friends wherever you are, for it contributes to your mental and spiritual health, and it contributes to your husband's ministry. A happy, emotionally healthy wife frees her husband from a lot of extra stress. Not least of all, it contributes to the ministry of the church. For whichever church has an adversary relationship with its minister's wife also has a weakened witness. She has to be happy and contented there, or it will begin to show up in a lot of places. If the minister and his wife only love people on the surface because they don't want to risk being hurt, what makes them think they can lead people in the church past surface relationships for each other?

This subject is more important than some might suppose. Ministers' wives are under a lot of pressure in this regard. Any weaknesses shown in their lives and shared with an ill-chosen friend could have lasting repercussions. It could ruin her husband's ministry in that place, so the minister's wife feels she's not free to make mistakes, to fall off that pedestal. If there's friction between the church and the minister's wife, there's also bound to be friction between the minister and his wife. She can either make him or break him. Her influence on him and for him should never be underestimated.

Obviously those ministers and wives who have short ministries have no time to wisely form close friendships. Since the average length of ministry in general is about three years, perhaps this reflects the great frustrations put upon the minister's family. A longer ministry affords the minister's family more time to slowly grow friendships and also enhances their feeling of security in ministry.

A "safe" outlet for close friendships can also be found in an area minister's wife or where there is a multiple ministry. Other ministers' wives on the same staff are kindred spirits. However, these should also be approached slowly and with caution. Sometimes jealousies develop over age factors, abilities, and acceptability within the church. These will cause unwise competition and limit your effectiveness and level of friendship. It is essential to earnestly pray for guidance and wisdom as you cope with this personal need of close friendships and its effect upon your ministry. Listen to what the Preacher says:

> Two are better than one: because they have a good reward for their labor. For if they fall, the one will lift up his fellow: but woe to him (or her) that is alone when he falleth; for he hath not another to help him up (Eccl. 4:9, 10, KJV).

REFLECTIONS

1. Do you think a minister's wife needs a close friend, or do you agree with the sentiment, "my husband is my best friend, and I don't need anyone else"? Why/why not?
2. Note reasons cited against forming close friendships in the church. Do you think reasons against this stem from concern for that close friend, or fear for the minister's wife herself? Why?
3. Do you agree with the alternative—for friendship outside the church? Why/why not?
4. Do you think that depression some ministers' wives are experiencing today might be linked to their loneliness and absence of close friends? Why?
5. How can a surface (superficial, non-binding) relationship between the minister's wife and the church help (or hinder) her effectiveness?
6. What steps might the minister's wife take in forming close friendships?

7. What things should be considered when cultivating friendships in a multiple-staff ministry?
8. Do you think ministers' wives are winners or losers when they refrain from forming close friendships in the church? How so?
9. How can prayer and reading God's word help in the selection of close friends?

SUGGESTED READING

The Care & Feeding of Ministers, "Fact and Fancy About Friends," by Kathleen Nyberg.
Be All You Can Be, "Can You Believe the Best of Your Friends?" by David Augsburger (Carol Stream: Creation House).
The Vision Splendid, "Loving a Congregation," by Dr. Paul Benjamin.

11

THE ART OF GIVING AND RECEIVING

The Happy Giver

Sooner or later in the life of the minister's wife, the subject of gift-giving arises. Most books for ministers' wives that deal with this subject counsel against giving gifts to those within the congregation. Reasons cited are that it might cause jealousy, it would be a financial burden, or that ministers' wives just don't want to give. If they don't get too close to people, it will relieve them of the obligation to give.

These apprehensions are easily understood. The minister's wife receives invitations to weddings, rehearsal dinners, bridal showers, baby showers, graduation parties, and family birthday and anniversary celebrations, etc. continuously. Immediately she must ask herself, "Is it proper to give a gift?" "Should I stay home so it won't be noticeable I'm not giving a gift?" "Will I be expected to give a gift?"

Some people the minister's wife may know well and want to give a gift; others she may not be well acquainted with and will not feel obligated to give, just as other individuals might do. Should she take a chance and give where she chooses, or must her title keep her from doing so? To choose not to give to anyone is, of course, the easiest thing to do. She can say, "Well, since I can't give to everyone, I won't give to anyone." But if she chooses this route, will she be robbing herself of the blessings of giving? Didn't Jesus say it was more blessed to give than to receive? (Acts 20:35) And Luke 6:38 states,

> Give and gifts will be given to you. Good measure, pressed down, shaken together, and running over, will be poured into your lap; for whatever measure you deal out to others will be dealt to you in return.

This verse also takes care of the financial worries over gift-giving. Isn't it wonderful that God has promised to give gifts to us in the same measure we give to others?! In fact, He will give abundantly to the givers. When we fail to be givers of gifts because "we don't have the finances" it may cause some to wonder if we really practice what we preach—that our God cares for all our needs and honors his promises.

The nature of our gift-giving will change with age. If we have no children or they are already away from the home, there are more monies available for "extras" such as this. If we have been good stewards we can usually squeeze gifts from our budgets, and rely on that which is in our hands. For younger families who still have the financial responsibilities which come from children in the home, buying gifts for extra occasions could be difficult. Are there any creative alternatives a minister's wife could employ which would enable her to be a giver too? Here we are only limited by our imaginations. Consider the following low-cost items as possible gift ideas:

- Make sachets from gingham or calico and fill with potpourri; then sew into a small pillow shape or tie like a small sack, using a pretty ribbon (wedding bell shapes, baby bootie shapes, hearts, etc.).
- Make drawer scents like the sachet pillows above, filling with cedar shavings.
- Make jellies or jams and put them in baby food jars. Cover lids with a gingham or calico material and tie with a ribbon.
- Make a party apron, potholders, or pillows if you are handy with a needle.

- Bread Dough Art—if you can bake, you can do this. Bake a loaf of bread, slowly baking until it is completely dry; then shellac and trim with a quaint bow for a table decoration.
- Establish a "happy box"; in this box put items you have bought at bargain prices. When a gift is needed, go to your "happy box" for it.
- If you can write poetry, write a poem for the occasion and attractively frame it.
- Go to your local library and check out some craft books. You'll be amazed at what you can do.
- Find a simple, yet clever Christmas ornament you can make, and use these for gift-giving.

One friend of mine buys a couple yards of flannel material and makes simple, but attractive baby receiving blankets, tying them with colored baby yarn. It has been said, "Where there's a will, there's a way," and that certainly applies to gift-giving. But first, we must deal with our own attitudes—do we really desire to give? I encourage you to prayerfully consider doing so. Then ask God for wisdom to handle it aright, and you'll be released from your imposed restrictions to be a happy giver. God loves that, you know! (See II Cor. 9:7.)

The Happy Receiver

It has been said that there are two kinds of people in this world today: the givers and the takers. Have you thought into which category you belong? Is it possible to fit into both of them? Because of her fears toward the dangers of gift-giving, the minister's wife may fall into the trap of expecting to receive many things (because she's the minister's wife), but not being expected to give in return (because she's the minister's wife). After practicing the "art of receiving" for so long, she comes to expect gifts at times. She is in danger of learning selfishness. The other extreme is the person who will receive nothing gracefully, because she doesn't want to feel obligated in any way. She then robs the giver of the blessings of giving.

Many years ago when we were in our first place of ministry, there was an old gentleman who would go out the church door each Sunday saying, "Preacher, I have an old rooster for you. He don't lay eggs too well, but he'll lay in the skillet just fine!'' This went on for many weeks. Then one evening as we were ready to leave for an appointment, we received a call to come at once to pick up the chicken. My husband drove to the address given and got the chicken. I'll never forget the expression on his face when he returned home and said, "Karen, you'll never believe it, but I have a rooster in a gunny sack as big as a turkey in the trunk! Would you believe it's alive?!'' It had been several years since my husband had skinned a squirrel and just as many since I had dressed out a chicken back on the farm, so you can imagine the laughable chicken pieces we finally came up with! (I realize now that we were before our time, for we're seeing similar chicken pieces in the store today!) This rooster was so big we had no kettles big enough for hot water to scald and pluck it. We had to dunk the top half first, boil more water and finish plucking the bottom half! I still giggle over that episode, for it's one of the most memorable gifts we've ever received! (I won't mention how long it took to cook, or if it ever got tender!) Just think of the fun we would have missed out on if we had refused to accept the gift.

Many people who participated in the Church Survey wrote that the minister's wife should attend more showers like the majority of church women do. Just what are they wanting from us when they express the desire for our attendance at these personal functions? I believe they are more interested in our attendance than in our gifts. They feel that we are honoring and accepting them as individuals when we bring ourselves and our gifts to them—just as we feel when they give gifts to us.

Gifts can be given for many reasons. They can be given to meet a particular need, as an apology, or as a gesture of gratitude or expression of love. They can be given for appeasement (Prov. 6:35) or to pacify anger (Prov. 21:14); sometimes they are given excessively, or to "buy" friendships (Prov. 17:23; Exod. 23:8). Proverbs 17:8 says gifts given and received should be regarded as "precious stones." All of us should strive to give in the spirit of love and to the glory of the greatest Gift-giver of all. (See John 3:27; James 1:17.) How can we possibly be in His image and not be givers of good gifts? Let us seek to recognize the needs that lie behind the gift-giving and move to meet those needs without rejecting the givers. Each gift we receive bears in it a bit of the giver's heart, so we need to guard against being insensitive to his feelings, or ungratefulness. Don't reject gifts whether you can or cannot use them, for God can help you find a way to utilize any gift. Try to receive them with gracious appreciation.

Let us look at our attitudes anew, and allow God to work in and through us in this area. We do need to learn the art of accepting gifts without feeling defensively that we will be beholden to the giver. Receive that gift in good faith as it comes from God. Keep foolish pride at bay. Remember, you are not responsible for the motive behind the gift you have received, but you are responsible for your attitude and the response you make when that gift is offered to you. Jesus is our example in this manner. He received both humble and extravagant gifts. He also gave humbly and extravagantly. St. Francis of Assisi said, ". . . it is in giving that we receive. . . ." Are we following Jesus in this matter of giving, or are we cheating ourselves of many of God's abundant blessings because we are not givers in word and deed?

Giving Through Hospitality

Is your church known as a hospitable church? Are you known as a hospitable minister? Do most members of the church practice hospitality or only a few? Do you have a tug of war in which the church claims it pays the minister to do this duty, and the minister and his wife retort there's hardly enough salary for themselves, let alone being "paid" for this extra expense—besides Scriptures list hospitality as a qualification for the office of an elder?! Is hospitality given grudgingly and on an "it's your turn now basis"?

While this might be the case in some churches, I am happy to report it is not the case in most churches. Of those who responded in the Church Survey, 22% agreed that it was the responsibility of the minister and his wife to extend hospitality to all who need it; 53% disagreed with that statement, and 26% wrote in that both the leadership and the ministers should share equally in this responsibility.

Results from the Minister's Wife Survey showed most of them enjoyed being hospitable. Some felt a financial hardship because they were expected to carry the whole church responsibility in this area. They wanted to be able to practice this gift freely, not because they were told it came with the job.

This subject of hospitality is two-pronged: it should be shared with those without the body, as well as within it. The minister's wife doesn't usually question whether or not she should extend hospitality to those visiting ministers, college students, missionaries, or those who request help. She knows it is a good thing and does it. But the question of whether or not she should invite those from within the church does bother her. She asks, "Would it cause jealousies and strife if I do so? Would it be proper to return dinner invitations, or will a small hostess gift in lieu of a return invitation be acceptable?"

Some ministers' wives feel they should not invite church people into their homes nor return dinner invitations. A growing number of them have sought to host members in their homes in the following ways: (taken from the Survey)

- Host Bible studies in their homes.
- Host Sunday School class socials, ladies' groups.
- Host spontaneous potluck dinners. For those last families who are standing around visiting after services she says, "Come on over and bring what you have."
- Yearly "Open House." This is a nice way to thank those who have opened their homes to the minister's family during the year.
- Popcorn or dessert after church in the evenings.
- Participate in dinner groups within the church.

One minister's wife wrote, "We entertain all our church members in our home. It took two years before we made our goal, but it has been the greatest blessing to us—our children are learning to be gracious hostesses. We all are enriched by that sweet fellowship and a wonderful open rapport has developed. It has also encouraged others to share in the same way in their homes. We have a great spirit of genuine, loving hospitality."

Doing something of this nature, of course, will be determined by the size of the congregation and the length of your ministry there.

The minister's house is a natural place to stop for the missionary traveling through, or coming to speak for the church. These people have much in common to discuss and share. There are two extremes in the minister's house. There are those who feel obligated to be hospitable since others aren't doing it. And there are those who selfishly dominate all the visiting dignitaries, and in the process rob others of the joy of hospitality and fellowship.

The Church Survey reflects that churches are becoming more aware of the need to shoulder this responsibility. Hopefully ministers will respond by sharing it with them.

While we do what we can about building up friendships in the church, let us not get so busy with those within that we neglect those without. Hospitality is a wonderful and powerful evangelical tool for non-church friends and neighbors. For when a person places his feet beneath your table, he finds out just what kind of a person you really are. He knows if you have a religion just in the head, or the practical kind in the heart as well. When you open your home to others you become vulnerable—others see the real you. What will they find at your house today? Will they find someone who is unwilling to share what God has provided, someone who is afraid to let her real self be seen, someone who resents having to expend her energies preparing a meal and cleaning a house for someone else?

Or will they find one who believes it is more blessed to give than to receive, one who is open and caring for others, one who will use her time and energy and resources for others in the name of Christ?

Be not forgetful to entertain strangers: for thereby some have entertained angels unawares (Heb. 13:2, KJV).

REFLECTIONS

1. Do you think it is proper for the minister's wife to give gifts to church members? Why/why not?
2. In what manner should ministers' wives receive gifts?
3. If lack of finances is used for not being liberal in our giving, what might be an inward problem?
4. Should church leaders function within a planned "hospitality plan" whereby visitors are entertained by various leaders, members, or should hospitality just be a spontaneous thing? Why?
5. Why is it sometimes difficult to get church people to be hospitable toward guests, or even one another?

6. Should finances govern our hospitality? Why?
7. Should ministers be free to invite individual members into their homes? Why?
8. Do church people and ministers sometimes neglect their neighbors and fellow workers because they're too busy with church work?

SUGGESTED READING

The Care & Feeding of Ministers, "A Chicken for the Sabbath Pot," by Kathleen Nyberg.

Open Heart, Open Home, by Karen Burton Mains (Elgin: David C. Cook Pub., 1976).

How to Be a Minister's Wife & Love It, "The Rectory Hilton," by Alice Taylor.

Underground Manual for Ministers' Wives, "The Hostess with the Leastest," by Ruth Truman (Nashville: Abingdon Press, 1974).

12

IS THE SALARY WORTHY
OF THE SERVANT?

Elders who do well as leaders should be reckoned worthy of a double stipend, in particular those who labour at preaching and teaching. For Scripture says, "You shall not muzzle a threshing ox"; and besides, "the worker earns his pay" (I Tim. 5:17, 18, NEB).

A few years ago there was talk about a certain group of ministers who threatened to unionize within their denomination. You can imagine the outcries, the uproar and protests over even just the thought! What do you suppose provoked them to even consider such a thing? Were they wanting more and more of the extras which they had seen in the homes of church members? Were their salaries just not keeping pace with the economy? Were churches expecting well-educated, experienced ministers to accept the pay of an uneducated laborer, or inexperienced novice? Were churches expecting ministers to take a vow of poverty like the priest, but with none of the accompanying advantages he has? This is a sore subject for many, and it surely needs to be examined more closely.

First let us look at the real attitudes in the churches today. Here is how they responded in the Survey regarding money-related issues:

- "The minister should be paid the average salary of the working men in the congregation, with similar fringe benefits."
RESPONSE: 65% Agreed; 30% Disagreed.
- "The minister's salary should reflect the average wage of the community, but also reflect his amount of education and years of service as in the business world.
RESPONSE: 79% Agreed; 17% Disagreed.

According to the Minister's Wife Survey, 55% said their salary was adequate for needs (not wants); 32% said it was inadequate; and 18% lived very frugally, often going without. Added to these statistics, 50% of those surveyed worked outside the home (of which 94% did so for financial reasons). Salary and parsonage had been used as a coercive bargaining tool on 24% of them, but for 76% it had not. This problem seemed to surface during their early years of ministry, and the later years of ministry. Here are some of their comments:

"I have often resented people's attitudes toward the minister's salary. They wanted to get the best man they could for the smallest amount of money. People seemed to feel that we should have a commitment to the ministry that would make us work for low wages. If we need more money, they think we aren't committed enough" . . . "We have barely enough but God provides in other ways" . . . "Our needs are met now, but retirement years are a constant nagging fear to my husband" . . . "We had to bare our souls and show our budget before we could get a raise" . . . "In some of my answers it sounds like money is everything, but that's not so. It would be nice to be able to have health insurance, a car that is reliable, and be able to buy shoes for the kids without wondering where the money will come from. We are not destitute or anything like that, but we can hardly make the bill payments for necessities."

Low salaries for the minister go hand in hand with a low feeling of self-worth. If a minister is habitually underpaid he will begin to have a feeling of low professional worth as well, and his work will show it.

The U.S. Department of Labor puts out a pamphlet listing occupations from the highest paid on down. In the 1976 report, clergymen ranked 317 out of the 432 occupations listed. That ranks them with the lowest paying occupations and with unskilled labor, such as farm laborers, waiters, and cooks. On the other hand, though they rank near the bottom economically, they rank educationally with the top-earning occupations such as lawyers, doctors, dentists, judges, college professors, etc. The Department of Labor, Bureau of Labor Statistics published the following information in the April, 1982 *Occupational Outlook Handbook,* 1982-1983 Edition:

> There were 230,000 protestant ministers actively serving in 1980. Their median income was approximately $15,000. An estimated 3,000 rabbis serving congregations earned $20,000 - $50,000 in 1980, with some senior rabbis in large congregations earning over $50,000 a year.

What is to become of our well-educated, poorly-paid ministers? And what about their wives who must cope with the effects of a low salary, making do with it, from the type of food they can afford to put on the table, to what clothing to put on the kids?

The minister must also cope with the accompanying headaches of a low salary. If he is preoccupied with pressing money problems it will hurt the effectiveness of his ministry. The minister who is underpaid is also cheated of the joy of being able to give liberally to the Lord and His work. Many times he is kept from earning a decent salary, not by ones who haven't much, but by those who have more than enough. What glory to the church and God is it if the minister is unable to pay his bills on time in the community? A minister who is known in the community as a poor credit risk directly reflects on the church.

Kathleen Nyberg in *The Care and Feeding of Ministers* says "a man is measured by the size of his salary in the eyes of the world— and after all, this is where ministers are working. Ministers can despise this fact, regret it, disavow it, yet it remains a fact of life. As a result the ministry has been steadily declining in status in the secular world.

For the sake of the world, if not the comfort of the minister, clergymen ought to be paid very well indeed."[1]

We hear much of the recurring theme that ministers are the same as lawyers and doctors. I wonder if some hospital has tried lately to hire a doctor and gets a receptionist (his wife) thrown in free; or if a factory worker takes a job in which he's expected to bring his wife along to help in the cafeteria? It is true they all have heavy demands on their time; however, doctors and lawyers receive compensation for long hours of overtime. The minister's salary is computed on a 40-hour week basis, with expectations of his working around the clock.

Low salaries can also contribute to the loss of our promising young men in the ministry profession. Some feel they can do more on the other side of the pulpit, and yet make a decent salary without all the hassle. They see no honor in being financially crippled. In the end, the church will suffer the most for lack of new ministers to replace the old and worn, or those leaving the ministry for another field.

Ministers are not the only ones who are abused financially. Some churches have been on the receiving end of poor treatment from ministers. I know of a church who settled a minister's accounts in another community before he would agree to come and minister with them. That was one of his requirements, along with a healthy raise for his trouble of moving. Another church paid around $5,000 as "unpaid back vacation pay" so a minister would leave the church quietly and cause no trouble; another minister promised to leave "quietly" if the church agreed not to audit its books! It is literally a crying shame that a few ministers have given a bad name to the majority, and churches are responding defensively. However, one bad minister doesn't make all ministers bad; similarly, one bad church doesn't make all churches bad. We are all individuals and need to be treated as such, not made to pay the price for the wrongs of someone else, be it church or minister.

What can be done about this for the sake of all concerned? To begin with, the churches could rethink their policy on salaries, and re-examine their attitudes. It is important to have a caring person chair the finance committee, not someone who considers church funds

---

1. Kathleen Neill Nyberg, *The Care and Feeding of Ministers* (Nashville: Abingdon Press, 1961), p. 73.

to be his own bag of gold to be spent and held back as he sees fit. Open communication is a must. Agreements between the minister and the congregation should be in writing *before* he moves on to the field. The temptation is too great to make promises which can't be delivered to entice him to move, then renege after he's moved because funds aren't available, or he didn't "understand what was promised." More than one motion has been made in regard to funds or benefits for the minister which were sent to a committee for action and languidly died. Such actions only promote distrust and cynicism in the minister. It would also be a good thing to periodically check on the minister after he has arrived, to see if his needs are adequately being met.

Church members (and Finance committees) need to be aware that the minister's workclothes are usually suits, not coveralls; that his car gets used for many church-related occasions, and drinks gas like it's going out of style; that study books and helps are expensive but necessary tools for the minister who wants to keep himself fresh; that many ministers and missionaries traveling through town stay overnight at the minister's home and eat at his table; that all church people enjoy receiving wedding, shower and baby gifts from the minister's family. To communicate these needs takes much courage and honesty. Rather than facing selfish church attitudes of "Should he get all that money for only one or two days of work a week?" the minister will suffer in silence, letting it eat away inside him. His pride may keep him from communicating his family's needs to the church. When their husbands won't speak up on behalf of the family's needs, some wives see their husbands as lacking in their manly duty toward providing adequately for them. Their bitterness begins to take its toll on that marriage. The wife may become cynical or bitter toward the church. Depression could become a real problem, along with disappointment and disillusionment with her marriage and the church.

On the other hand, many good things can come about when we are forced to turn to the Lord for help that none else give. Our faith grows when we can't do things ourselves, and our chidlren have an opportunity to see faith in action. It is true that out of adversity can come blessing, even when the financial squeeze is on. We learn to manage our money better; our kids aren't spoiled by having too many "things." We learn to develop our creative skills and make things rather than buy them. We begin to make proper decisions regarding finances. We learn how to make money work for us, rather than our working for it. We learn to cope with negative attitudes created by stress. If we have been cheated of the joy of giving more liberally, we find new ways to give that don't necessarily include a monetary gift. We learn to give time, or talent, or influence, or something which we already have in our possession. If we have resentment for those who force sacrificial giving upon us, we can learn to direct that gift toward God and not for the benefit of man.

It is right for ministers and their wives to learn to be content in whichever state they are. It is wrong for churches to patronize preachers, to purposely underpay them, then claim they're actually helping God teach them humility and dependence.

Although we must work with and answer to the leadership in the local church, God is "employer" to us all, and He's promised to never leave us or forsake us if we strive to please Him. There is great security in knowing that. We must remember that God will call us all to an accounting in this matter—both minister and church. It is good to note that the Minister's Wife Survey reflected the fact that most ministers are service-oriented. They accept hardships and make sacrifices for the cause of Christ. If this weren't true, half the pulpits across our land would probably be vacant. Let us keep foremost before us the charge from Colossians 3:23, 24:

> Whatever you are doing, put your whole heart into it, as if you were doing it for the Lord and not for men, knowing that there is a Master who will give you your heritage as a reward for your service.

REFLECTIONS

1. Do you think ministers in general, are paid enough for their labor? Why/why not?
2. Does your minister's salary reflect the average wage of the community, including his amount of education and experience? Why?
3. What might happen when a minister is paid inadquately?
4. Is there any relationship between a poorly paid minister and his effectiveness in the church or community? Explain.
5. Do you think those outside the church would respect the church more if it took better care of its ministers? Why/why not?

6. What are some constructive things a church can do financially for the minister?
7. What can be done to alleviate distrust over finances which stems from bitter experiences of the past from ministers or churches?
8. What attitude should the minister and his family have regarding finances?

SUGGESTED READING

They Cry Too, by Lucille Lavender.

Divorce in the Parsonage, "Money Problems," by Mary LaGrand Bouma.

Underground Manual for Ministers' Wives, "The Love of Money Is Sin," by Ruth Truman.

The Care & Feeding of Ministers, "The Evil Root Bears Beautiful Blossoms," by Kathleen Nyberg.

13

THE PREACHER AND THE PARSONAGE

In the last twenty years many churches have opted to go out of the "housing business" by including housing allowance in the minister's salary and encouraging him to buy his own home. These churches sometimes use the former parsonage for office or classroom space. They may sell the house or move it in order to use the lot for parking space. Control of where the minister lives, or saving money on his salary by providing his housing isn't quite as sought after as it used to be. This seems to be happening in all denominations. Churches are beginning to question the feasibility of a church-owned parsonage in these days.

The Church Survey revealed that 78% of the people did not think it is better for a church to provide a parsonage and include that in the minister's wage; 84% thought it was better to let the minister choose to rent or buy his own house just as church members have that choice. There are benefits as well as hindrances both from the point of view of the church and the minister.

ADVANTAGES FOR A CHURCH-OWNED PARSONAGE include:

- The church may determine the type of housing and area in which their minister lives. This protects them from possible public embarrassment if he should choose to live in a low-income area (making it look like he is poorly paid), or in a high income area (where some might think he was "above himself" or might limit his effectiveness with the comman man).
- When the house is paid for, the church eventually saves money, at the same time ensuring the minister a nice place to live—provided of course, that they have maintained the property well.
- Having a house available enables a minister to move onto the field more quickly, instead of having to wait until suitable housing is found.
- Sometimes the lot for a parsonage can be purchased at a great savings along with land for a new building; thus it is available for utilization.
- Parsonages are often seen as additional space for classrooms and meetings by some church members—but proves a source of irritation to the minister's family if used in this manner.
- Many times major appliances and draperies are furnished by the church, which cuts down expense for the minister. (This can also be done if the church desires to help when the minister buys or rents his own home.)
- Less outlay of cash for the church. If they provide a parsonage, they can pay him less in salary.

As you can see, most of the advantages are for the church rather than for the minister.
DISADVANTAGES OF A CHURCH-OWNED PARSONAGE include:

- The church does not determine the area or type of housing for the minister. Church members and community people all have distinct ideas about where the minister should live. Some think he should live in a home as nice as the church members own. They want the community to think well of them. Some think it should be as good as the average church home (who determines what is average?); not as nice as their most affluent members have, but not as bad as their poorer members have. Others think he should live as cheaply as possible—not above anyone else in case he gives offense. They vote for a "Humility House."

Several years ago we moved from a congregation with a parsonage to one which offered a housing allowance. At the time we were under obligation to pay several hospital bills, so we chose a simple "prefab" house to enable us to liquidate our debts. One lady was disappointed that we were going to live in an area where the houses were rather cheap and all looked the same. She thought we should live in something more grand that was more fitting to our social standing.

Community people have certain expectations, too. While looking for a home to buy in one community, the realtor chose from her listing what she thought was "suitable" for us. She was reluctant to show us older houses. I enjoy decorating them because of their uniqueness and wanted to view several of them, but somehow she didn't think that was the proper housing for our needs. The community does measure the church to some extent by the house in which their minister lives.

- Some people will take advantage of the parsonage. They may consider it public property for any church use. Stories abound of misuse of the parsonage kitchen, bathroom, yard, etc. The temptation is also to abuse the minister's privacy and time schedule (at all hours) if the parsonage is close to the church building. Family meals can be constantly interrupted for church keys, or to borrow something that isn't in the church kitchen. If the minister's study is in the home, it is hard to separate work time from family time. People come for counseling and it's hard to keep the children quiet, or people leave their kids for the minister's wife to care for while they talk to the minister.
- A parsonage can be misused as a "pressure point" to keep the minister and his family in line. Many times the parsonage has served as a battleground between the minister's wife and the church, with the poor minister caught in the crossfire! Needed repairs have often been put off until a more convenient time, or until the minister's wife comes to heel.

121

- Many parsonages are over twenty years old, and heat expenses are very draining on the minister's salary, whereas a newer, better insulated house would cost less for upkeep and repairs.
- The minister who is not a home-owner has no chance to build up equity in his property for future retirement. He also has no borrowing power without property. If the minister's wife becomes a widow she has no security to fall back on. How long will the congregation be able to allow her to live in the parsonage? How long will she receive her husband's salary?! Many churches do not want her to work outside the home, so there will be no Social Security benefit to draw on. When a new minister moves onto the field and she must leave the parsonage, where will she go? Many ministers may be falsely accused of being discontent with their lot, and of loving possessions (a house) when in reality all they want to do is care for and make provisions for their own, which is commendable in any circumstance. This seems to be a serious problem in independent churches where they are not required to send a certain amount of money to "headquarters" for the minister's retirement fund. Usually ministers are not paid well enough to save much for retirement either; they have their needs met and that's about all. Mainline denominations contribute to a pension fund; Catholic churches provide places for priests and nuns at retirement, but the independent minister seems to have no place to lay his head when he retires. This group is sadly lacking in retirement provisions for its ministers. There are several isolated cases where churches provide commendably and adequately, but this is not the case with the majority. Wouldn't it be a good thing to care for your own after they've given a lifetime in service to the church and to Christ? Ministers who have this responsibility lifted from their shoulders by loving, caring churches are much more effective for the church and the Kingdom.
- Ministers who move from one church to the next during depressed housing markets are apt to be making double house payments for a sustained length of time, whether or not they have adequate salary. This is quite a disadvantage for the minister owning his own house. What happens if a church extends the call to a

minister (home-owner), he accepts the call, moves to the new location and then finds he can't sell his former home? What if he gets to the place financially that he cannot pay his bills in the community because of the double house payments? Should the minister resign from his job with the church and seek a secular job until his financial obligations are taken care of? Is the church morally obligated to help him financially with a gift or loan which could be paid back upon the sale of his other house? This is a sticky question to be sure, but one that should be discussed when a church calls the minister to come. The possibility of owning two homes for an extended length of time could become a reality. A caring, loving church will be alert to the needs of the minister, and seek to help him work through a financial problem such as the above, for the tremendous amount of financial pressure on him can sap his energy and certainly affect his work in the church.

Sometimes a minister will move into a new community and choose to rent a house rather than buy one, especially if he is still the proud owner of one he left behind. It should not be misconstrued that he isn't buying because he doesn't want to put down roots. More likely, he just cannot afford a down payment along with all the extra expenses, new licenses, and utility deposits that come with moving.

When the church offers a housing allowance, it removes the tenant/landlord relationship, along with all the possible temptations for coercion and complaints. It removes a possible battleground between the minister's family and the church. The minister is then free to take care of needed repairs and upkeep without complaining to the property committee for its laxness in getting jobs done. If he can't afford it, then he's like other homeowners—he learns to choose financial priorities as others must do.

Any possible harmony on this subject hinges on two things: attitudes and communication. The attitude of the church and minister must both focus on what is best for all concerned. The church should not save money at the expense of the minister, leaving him to swing on his own. Neither should the minister make impossible demands, gleefully writing his own ticket for all his fondest wishes. Both parties should take into account what is best for all concerned.

Communication between the church and the minister's family is crucial, and not just in this area of concern. Many times hard feelings arise because only a few on a property committee pull the strings and call the shots regarding the parsonage. They do not always reflect the feelings of the majority. One minister's wife wrote, "Our biggest problem here is the heat expense in this big house. The church pays it but the treasurer and his wife always act like it comes out of their pocket and she doesn't miss an opportunity to let me know how high the bills are." With a housing allowance some sources of friction such as this can be removed. The parsonage kitchen only needs one mother, and when there are many, the sparks begin to fly.

Church committees need to communicate when they will do needed repairs, improvements and etc., so the parsonage family can plan around them. There are some thoughtful property committees who go so far as to ask the minister's wife what her favorite paint color is, and will occasionally replace old carpet with new. These people are certainly to be commended for their caring spirit.

A note of warning: we as ministers' wives must learn that our security comes from Who owns our lives, rather than whether or not we have the freedom to own our own homes. Let us accent how we live, rather than where we live, and be able to say with the Apostle Paul, "for I have learned in whatsoever state I am, therewith to be content" (Phil. 4:11).

REFLECTIONS

1. Do you think the church should retain the right to decide what type of housing the minister has? Why?
2. What are some advantages of the church-owned parsonage (for both minister and church)?
3. What are some disadvantages of a parsonage, for both minister and church?
4. What are some advantages when the minister has the choice of home ownership (for both minister and church)?
5. What are some disadvantages of a preacher-owned house, for both preacher and church?
6. Do you think the community forms an opinion of the church and minister by his type of housing? How so?

7. How might the parsonage be used in a coercive way, both by the minister and the church? Is it right?
8. How should a property committee function in relationship to the parsonage and the minister's family?
9. What options does a church and minister have when as a home-owner he is called to a new place of ministry, only to be saddled with a house he cannot sell as he's trying to also buy one in the new location? Any creative solutions?

SUGGESTED READING

The Care & Feeding of Ministers, "Anybody Home?" by Kathleen Nyberg.

Underground Manual for Ministers' Wives, "Parsonage Roulette," by Ruth Truman.

14

A WORD TO THE CONGREGATION

This book would be incomplete if it were to deal only with one side of the relationship between the minister's family and the congregation. To do so would be like the marriage counselor who only talks to one partner. It is much more effective when both parties are included in the solution process. This chapter, then, is for you, dear church member.

Are there any ways in which you can particularly minister to your minister's wife which would enable her to be a more effective wife and mother, and in the process enhance her ministry with you and for you? Yes, you can make a definite contribution in this regard. Here are some ways you can minister to your minister's wife:

Encourage Her (Matt. 7:12)

- If your church owns a parsonage, encourage her by being a good landlord. Take care of necessary painting and repairs so she doesn't have to embarrassingly keep asking for things to be taken care of. Regard the parsonage as the minister's home and respect

127

their need for privacy, rather than using the parsonage as if it were yours, borrowing from them frequently, and robbing them of their privacy.

- Encourage her by respecting her need for family life. Don't expect her or her husband to be out every night of the week doing "church work." Don't interrupt their evenings with unnecessary phone calls that can be taken care of during office hours. Expect that she will want and need to spend time with her husband and children, and gently encourage her to do so if she is in danger of over-extending herself by taking on too many church responsibilities. Encourage her to also spend time during holidays, if possible, with their families back home, to nurture and build up these relationships as well.

Mary Bouma, author of *Divorce in the Parsonage,* points out the importance of your encouragement in this matter when she writes, "Ralph Heynen, who has counseled hundreds of pastors and their wives in almost thirty years as chaplain in a Christian psychiatric hospital, says, 'The variety and intentsity of work required of the modern clergyman demand much of his energy and time. Often this leads to the neglect of his family. . . . The pastor's wife and children, too, have needs that must be met. They have no pastor to whom they can go; they have only an absentee husband and father. A number of the drop-outs from the ministry have resulted from the choice made by a pastor's wife, rather than first of all the choice of her husband.'"[1]

- Encourage her by paying her husband an adequate salary, so she is not constantly harrassed with "making do" for her family. Ask yourself if he is paid according to his education and experience. Is he paid below the income level of professional people in the congregation, and embarrassed when he can't participate in activities with other church members because of lack of finances? Would you be willing to work his hours with the demands upon his time and abilities for his pay?
- Encourage her and her husband by giving them the time off, and the necessary resources to attend retreats, refresher courses,

---

1. Mary LaGrand Bouma, *Divorce in the Parsonage* (Minneapolis: Bethany Fellowship, 1979), p. 44.

marriage enrichment programs, conventions and seminars which would build them back up again, and cause them to be more effective in their ministry with you and to you. This will help prevent staleness and ministry "burn-out," and their quality of ministry with you will be directly affected.

• Encourage her by praying for her and her family daily. Do you realize the extra stress and demands of her position? Satan works overtime on the minister's wife and family, for their influence extends over a great many people. He knows that if the shepherd falls, the sheep will follow. So diligently pray for them all.

• Encourage her verbally. If you love her, tell her so. Don't wait until she moves to another place to tell her she is loved. She needs to know it now.

• Encourage her to develop her role in the community as family situations allow. She is a many-faceted person just as you are: she has a place in the community just by virtue of the fact that she is married to your minister. Encourage her to be involved in some community activities, so long as her family and church relationships will not suffer. She needs to grow in this area of her life as well. She will make a wonderful field representative for the church in the community, wherever her influence can be felt.

Love Her Unconditionally (Matt. 7:12)

Well now, how can you do that? Do you mean love her warts and all?! Yes, that's exactly what I do mean!

• Love her for herself alone. Let her be free from the stereotyped expectations of the congregation. Let her be free to express her true talents in areas of her own choosing in the church—not just those unwanted jobs which no one else will do. Realize there is a time and season for all things (Eccl. 3) and allow her room for her "seasons," to function in different areas at different times in her life.

Love her enough to let her be herself. You weren't expecting Kathryn Hepburn, Doris Day and Golda Meier all rolled up into one, were you? You realize of course, she's just like you. After all, she came from one of your families, and one of your churches. Treat her as an individual, but also understand the extra expectations thrust upon her because of whom she married. Realize how emotionally tied she is to the church. If things don't go well in the church, your husband isn't likely to lose his job, but hers could very easily.

Don't compare her with the last minister's wife who may have been older or younger than she is. If she is older, she will probably have more time to devote to the church; if she is younger, she may have more home and family obligations which would come before outside activities. She may be a young Christian as well as a young wife, who has been thrust into the role of Minister's Wife, which would even make older women with more years of growth and experience tremble at the thought of it. Love her for herself and give her room to grow and make mistakes. Don't expect her to know in five years what it took you twenty years to learn.

- Love her family. Love and respect her husband for his ministry with you. If you have a difference of opinion, go to him personally and don't use her as a sounding board or battering ram to get to him. Give her kids room to grow also. Don't expect them to live by a different set of standards than your kids do. It's hard for children to grow up in a glass house and not be expected to put on some kind of show for that ever-watching audience. Be tender and loving with them.
- Love her enough to let her develop personal friendships. This really takes mature loving, for she may not choose you for that close friendship. It may be someone more her age and with similar interests. For her mental and emotional well-being, she needs this freedom—don't rob her of it. Remember that Jesus also had a need for close friendships, and so does she.
- Love her like a member of your own family. When she married a minister, this is one of the things she had to give up to follow him. She left her parents, grandparents, sisters, brothers, and other relatives behind. She misses out on all those warm family get-togethers and special holidays. Will you be her "family"

130

there? Sometimes the very nature of her position and ministry sets her apart in a lonely place. Will you help bridge the gap and include her? Get to know her as a person; remember her on special days like birthdays, anniversaries, Valentine's Day. Let her know you appreciate her as you do a member of your own family. Love her as a daughter, a sister, a mother.

• Love her enough to admonish her. Now, wait a minute, did I really say that? Yes, I really did! To admonish means "to warn or caution GENTLY; to reprove MILDLY." But is there really a need for this in the church today? Yes, there is a need for this in the whole church body, as well as for the minister's wife. Fortunate indeed is the young minister's wife who is gently taken aside by a loving older woman and counseled wisely when the need arises. Let me stress that it should be an older woman; and the only motivation should be of love for the younger minister's wife, and love for the church. If it is done after much prayer and consideration, and as a mother who seeks to "bring them up (help them grow up spiritually) in the nurture and admonition of the Lord," she may well have saved that minister's ministry, and kept at bay some vicious hurtful gossip which might have inflicted lasting damage to his wife. Scripture gives us some definite guidelines in this area:

> A fool thinks that he is always right; wise is the man who listens to advice (Prov. 12:15).

And here's the way in which we should admonish each other: Romans 15:4 encourages us to be full of goodness and knowledge and to admonish one another. It is a foregone conclusion that if you admonish without goodness and knowledge, a great furor will arise. II Thessalonians 3:15 says this should be done as brothers, and not as enemies. Colossians 3:15 & 16 read, "Let Christ's peace be arbiter in your hearts; to this peace you were called as members of a single body. And be filled with gratitude. Let the message of Christ dwell among you in all its richness. Instruct and admonish each other with the utmost wisdom" (NEB).

It takes a real mature loving to admonish another when you may be rejected yourself for doing so. Don't let your pride be greater than your love for your minister's wife.

Help Her (Matt. 7:12)

- First of all, help her by example. Be an example to her as to how she should behave. According to Titus 2, the older women were admonished to set a high standard of conduct for the younger women, teaching them in conduct toward their husbands, their children and the community. They were to teach them to be chaste, kind, busy at home and to respect the authority of their own husbands. Obviously, an older woman who did not do these things herself, would not make a suitable teacher or example. This admonition from Titus encompasses every area in which the wife lives.
- Help her by teaching her. This is especially aimed at the younger ministers' wives. You older women have a responsibility not only of setting an example in conduct, but also actively teaching and admonishing the younger woman so she will be what God wants her to be. Are you letting God work through you so that you can help the younger minister's wife in this way?
- Help her with extra responsibilities she may have because of her position. As stated before, there are many invitations and demands upon her time. You might volunteer every now and then to babysit with her children while she attends a shower or committee meeting or whatever. You might even babysit so she can have a night out with her husband. Two dear older ladies had this as a ministry to all ministers' wives in one of the churches we served. They didn't have much money to give to the church, but they could give time, and considered it a ministry to us. How blessed we were by them. What young minister's wife wouldn't welcome a grandma or aunt to wrestle with her young children on the back row at church while Dad is in the pulpit? She may retain more hair and hear more sermons if you go to her rescue when the need arises!
- Help her by not monopolizing her time. Give her time to be with other people too. Ask yourself, "If she spent as much time with

132

others as I think she should spend with me, would there be time for other people and other responsibilities?''

As you can see from this chapter, the role your minister's wife plays is not one-sided; your attitude is also important. You can both enhance each other's ministry: you need each other. You can make her more effective, and especially lighten her load by encouraging her in many ways, loving her uncondtionally, and by helping her. As Galatians 6:2 says, ''Carry each other's burdens, and in this way you will fulfill the law of Christ.''

In closing, listen to these words of the Apostle Paul:

> Now if your experience of Christ's encouragement and love means anything to you, if you have known something of the fellowship of his Spirit, and all that it means in kindness and deep sympathy, do make my best hopes for you come true! Live together in harmony, live together in love, as though you had only one mind and one spirit between you. Never act from motives of rivalry or personal vanity, but in humility think more of one another than you do of yourselves. None of you should think only of his own affairs, but each should learn to see things from other people's point of view (Phil. 2:1-4, Phillips Translation).

REFLECTIONS

1. In what ways can church members encourage the minister's wife?
2. How can church members love the minister's wife unconditionally?
3. Is there a time to admonish the preacher's wife? If so, when should it be done and who should do it?
4. What ways can church members help the minister's wife?
5. Do you think the role of minister's wife is largely her attitude toward that role, or is the church's attitude also important? Why or why not?

SUGGESTED READING

Divorce in the Parsonage, ''Words to Congregations,'' by Mary LaGrand Bouma.

BIBLIOGRAPHY

Benjamin, Paul. *The Vision Splendid* (Washington, D. C.: National Church Growth Research Center, The American Press, 1981).

Bouma, Mary LaGrand. *Divorce in the Parsonage* (Minneapolis, Minn.: Bethany Fellowship, Inc., 1979).

Christenson, Larry and Nordis, Iverna Tompkins, Jamie Buckingham: "The Divorce Dilemma," *Logos Journal,* Nov./Dec., 1978.

Dobson, James A. *Hide or Seek* (Old Tappan, N.J.: Fleming H. Revell Co., 1979).

Dobson, James A. (An interview with) "Snatching the Family From Its Grave," *Christianity Today,* May, 1982.

Ensworth, George. "Notice the Divorced Among Us," *Christianity Today,* May 1982.

Gee, Opal Lincoln. "Creative Criticism," *Christian Standard,* May 1, 1983.

Lavender, Lucille. *They Cry Too* (New York: Hawthorne Books, 1976).

Mace, David and Vera. *What's Happening to Clergy Marriages?* (Nashville: Abingdon Press, 1980).

Malcolm, Kari Torjesen. *Women at the Crossroads* (Downers Grove, Il.: InterVarsity Press, 1982).

Nyberg, Kathleen Neill. *The Care and Feeding of Ministers* (Nashville: Abingdon Press, 1961).

Swindoll, Charles R. *Killing Giants, Pulling Thorns* (Portland: Multnomah Press, 1978).

Taylor, Alice. *How to Be a Minister's Wife and Love It* (Grand Rapids: Zondervan Publishing House, 1968).

Tournier, Paul. "The Secret of True Harmony," *Leadership,* Fall, 1981.

Turner, Denise D. "You Mean That's the Minister's Wife?" *Your Church,* Nov./Dec., 1979.

GUIDE FOR THE PREACHER'S WIFE

	AGREE	DISAGREE	NOT SURE
1. The minister's wife should be a leader for the women in the congregation in appearance and conduct....................	55%	41%	2%
2. It is important for a preacher's wife to attend most church functions, and all of the women's functions .... (Depends on age of kids)	38%	20%	3%
3. The preacher's wife should have some Bible college education	48%	41%	5%
4. Assuming salary is adequate, the preacher's wife should not work outside the home	51%	36%	8%
5. Ideally, the preacher's wife should have musical ability........................	35%	56%	2%
6. The role of a preacher's wife should be one of standing behind her husband, encouraging him, rather than taking an active part in leading....................... (Both 7%)	67%	23%	
7. A preacher's wife should act as a "sounding board" and go-between for congregation and minister	12%	78%	3%
8. The preacher's wife is considered at the hiring of her husband, and should therefore "fill in" for him when he is not available .... (Both 1%)	11%	82%	1%
9. The preacher's wife should be prepared to help in counseling people in the church ... (If talented here 5%)	47%	43%	2%
10. It is a good thing for the preacher's wife to form close friendships within the local church .... ("No favorites"; "yes, but not clannish"; "to a degree")	77%	14%	6%
11. The minister should definitely take a regular day off and church members should respect his need to do so	90%	5%	1%
12. The minister and his wife should consider themselves to be co-laborers together with the church members, working with them, not for them .... (Both 2%)	95%	2%	5%

	AGREE	DISAGREE	NOT SURE
13. The preacher's wife should only be expected to volunteer for or work in those areas in which her talents and abilities lie, letting others do jobs which do not fit into this category	77%	16%	2%
(No more than others 1%)			
14. The minister's salary should reflect the average wage of the community, but also reflect his amount of education and years of service (as in the business world)	76%	15%	4%
(Up to elders 5%)			
15. It is better for the church to provide a parsonage and include that in the minister's wage...............................	32%	46%	
(Between elders and minister 11%)			
16. The minister and his wife should be encouraged (financially) to attend seminars and retreats to better equip themselves for ministry............................	91%	2%	5%
17. The minister and his wife should be tithers...............................	88%	12%	5%
(Between them and God 3%)			
18. The minister and his wife should feed and house visiting speakers and evangelists ...	21%	53%	
(no more than others share it 21%)			
19. The preacher's wife should ignore criticism of her husband and keep it to herself.....	30%	53%	5%
(Depends on situation 6%)			
20. When criticized herself, the preacher's wife should not seek to defend herself or confront her accuser, she should let the matter drop to avoid problems..........	27%	54%	7%
(Depends - what would Jesus do? 3%)			
21. The preacher's wife should know office skills so she can be of assistance to her husband in the church office	19%	65%	6%
(Helps in smaller churches 1%)			
22. The preacher's wife should know her Bible well and be able to teach	77%	27%	
(If talented here 3%)			

	AGREE	DISAGREE	NOT SURE

23. The preacher's wife should not accept a position of leadership (such as choir director or president of the Ladies' Circle) where she would be in the public eye; rather her role should be one of supporting others ..   32%   52%   7%
    (Up to her 2%)

24. Would you encourage your son to become a minister or your daughter to marry one? Why or why not?
    Yes - 48%; No - 5%; Their choice - 4%; Did not know, not sure - 16%

25. What do you think the average length of a ministry should be? Check one:
    1-3 years - 3%; 4-6 years - 10%; 7-10 years - 19%; over 10 - 23%; N/a 29%;
    Long as successful - 3%; Led by the spirit - 13%

26. If you were giving advice to a young minister's wife as she and her husband start their first ministry, what three things would you consider important for her to know from the standpoint of one within the congregation? List in order of importance.

    Top vote getters were:

    1. Be yourself - be happy and content and don't try to please everyone.
    2. Keep your priorities straight - have God first in your life.
    3. Support, help, listen to, encourage husband (a good wife is the making of good preachers).
    4. Be friendly, kind to all.